The House Th

By Davi

ISBN:
9781686151507

The House That Dave Built

Contents

This book is dedicated to two people who inspire me with life, purpose, and humour. My girlfriend Joanna and daughter, Rebecca.

They inspired me to write my experiences down and also turn writing into a pastime which I enjoy as a calm and quieter adventure.

Disclaimer – Whilst this is a true story, names and details have been changed in order to protect identities of those involved. Some events have been omitted or removed due to prevent legal issues. Everything else can be backed up by evidence such as photographs, video, eye witness testimony and official records. Some laws and procedures will have naturally changed in the time between my building experience and writing this book so don't rely on any laws, practices or procedures mentioned without consulting the appropriate experts. I hope you enjoy this book simply for enjoyment of a good story.

Special thanks to Joanne Hodson and David Matthews for their exceptional, invaluable and careful attention to detail.

Other titles due out soon are:

'A Dishonest Code' - more details at www.adishonestcode.com

'A Thoroughly Modern Treasure Hunt' - more details at www.adishonestcode.com

Other releases are available from Big Hits Publishing - more details at www.bighitspublishing.com

Chapter 1 – An Introduction

"Building your own home is about desire, fantasy. But it's achievable; anyone can do it."

Kevin McCloud, TV presenter of home building show 'Grand Designs', May 2014

No it's not Kev.

I'd rather swim in shark infested waters on a holiday with no travel insurance, with both my hands tied behind my back and with the juiciest piece of tuna John West could find in my mouth. Or eat a tray of chocolate brownies, then discover they were stool samples... collected from the dog... for the vet.

Or play lucky dip with a bag of... well, I think you get the idea.

July 2018.

It has been four years since I embarked on the biggest threat of my life to my financial security and mental health. The scars are only just healing and my penfriend at the bank has only just stopped writing letters. This is the true tale of the house built by Dave - that's me. And how building my own home bulldozed my finances and played Twister with my sanity. My story follows the chaotic and at times comedic episodes of how to build your own home. And how everything from planning permission to first occupation of my home fell regularly, and with a certain inevitability, into every pitfall available. From regular police visits, council investigations, panic at the bank, meddling neighbours, suppliers who think a deadline is a start line, burning furniture and to the accidental ability to create significant gas explosions, the new self-build experiences were darkly entertaining.

This is my story. The story of an 'average Joe' backed by a budget far less than the typical Grand Design TV show contestants with the casual £500k to throw around. Or the smug entrepreneur with mere millions lying around for a pet building project. I had a modest and almost recklessly tiny budget backed by a teacher's salary. A teacher's salary so small that raising my family in the bedroom of my parents' home was a very real possibility unless I did something sooner rather than later. My solution was to build my very own house and short cut my way to the dream home. This is a story of an ordinary man in the street, relentlessly marching towards his own financial Armageddon and with a lot to learn. This is the story about how my life got turned upside down.

Some of the names in this story have been changed to protect the identities of those involved and events edited to avoid funding more law firms. I've helped barristers enjoy more than their fair share of exotic holidays to destinations around the world. Holidays so expensive I'd never heard of most of the locations I'd paid for. However, the images on Facebook and Instagram looked great. To avoid funding more luxury excursions for my legal buddies or my law insurance broker becoming a broken man this is the true story of trying to self-build a home with just a few details changed. As much as possible the technical and legal knowledge was up-to-date when my home was built but don't take my word for it. Ask an expert because this novice could be wrong or has simply forgotten in the building whirlwind and mists of time.

My story of building a home will hopefully guide other would-be builders with cautionary tales, useful ideas and with hindsight how to do things better. For others the story of an average Joe building his own home on a modest budget against the odds might inspire and motivate you to follow more safely and informed in my footsteps. For other readers I hope my story will entertain you, move you or make you smile. I'll explain how an average Joe can be thrown through more emotions of hope, fear, anxiety and excitement than the entire cast of Coronation Street could muster on a blockbuster Christmas cliff hanger. I'm not asking you to walk in my shoes; I'd never wish my afflictions on anyone. But as you join me on my entertaining building adventures I'd like to start by recommending useful advice I learnt the hard way.

My self-build home plan was simple in theory – take an old barn on the family farm and convert it into a modern home. The barn would leap from its ruined state to a modern home complete with driveway, its first electric conveniences, heating by gas and fresh water delivered by pipe. What could be easier? I would build an affordable home in the depths of an expensive countryside that only offers homes for those whose bank cards didn't make a funny sound at the supermarket tills. I just needed a plan and budget.

When you take all of your worldly belongings, life savings and the huge effort you need to successfully build your own home you're going to need help. You're going to learn a huge amount. You'll need to master everything from building foundations to fitting windows. You'll become an expert at adding slates to your roof and building kitchen units from plans which make a NASA space launch look easy. You'll also need actual 'been there, done that' knowledge from experts. The sort of experience and knowledge that can't be learnt in the pub from your friend *'Baz'* or *'Gaz'* or from videos on YouTube. And unless you have the biceps of Arnold Schwarzenegger, the legal knowledge of Judge Rinder and the diplomacy skills of the United Nations you are going to need friends for support.

My local builder would be the ringmaster of my circus and would do the skilled parts of the building work. I would organise the rest. To keep costs down I would do as much labouring as possible in between my days as a teacher. The builder was an older man of few words, he had a strong grasp of overcoming the difficult and a respected command of his team and family who made up his staff. He had a reputation for excellent workmanship. He was also the only builder with the will to take on an underfunded, tall order project with disaster written all over it. He was (and still is) a legend to me.

My friend and construction expert from university was Ross. He was an enthusiast of all things building and had a calm knowledge beyond his years. Ross lived and breathed electrics, draining, wall insulation, damp proofing and anything else he'd learnt in his own massive flat renovating project. He was also a genius at finding bargain basement prices for anything and everything using eBay. His ideas saved money. And, his experiences ensured he got a lot of phone calls from me to find fixes to my building problems. Good advice is worth its weight in gold.

Advice number one; you should watch the pennies to save the pounds on any building project as you would in life. Unless of course you are Bill Gates; in which case you'd need more than one lifetime to spend your way into poverty. For me there were some costs my limited budget would need to strip away. People such as project managers or architectural service agents such as building site managers would be put in the dustbin of luxury add-ons. These services were unnecessary expenses. Project managers or architectural management services usually charge ten percent of your total build budget. Cutting these services was a huge saving for me. After all, I could manage the project. I only lived a hundred metres away from the barn at my parents' farmhouse. Being on a tight budget the slashing of these services from my planning was easy. Only later would I learn why ten percent for co-ordination of suppliers, raw material delivery and managing trades was something professional builders were willing to accept. Again I have no desire to suffer twice, in reality and then in retrospect, so I'll move on. There are a lot of tasks to plan.

Some tasks such as electrics and gas work you'll want to do yourself but legally you have no chance. By all means change a lightbulb or a fuse but don't go crazy on cost cutting and enter into activities such as wiring up to the national grid yourself unless you enjoy lethal accidents or a lengthy prosecution. If something did go wrong your building insurer could walk away with a smug grin should you burn your home down without official electric and gas installation certificates. Work such as installing gas and electric to a property needs to be done correctly and this means parting with some money. Beyond heavy machinery or laying slates on a high roof they are also two of the few ways you can have a serious accident within seconds. Just to balance this out and make you feel cheerful again you can paint the insides of your home in as many bright colours as you like and plant flowers anywhere. There are no laws against these...yet.

In building, ideas are important and even more important is that they work. Good ideas are like trainers – they simply work. For good ideas and true innovation you need human interaction, argument and debate. Too many ideas and the plan can be messy. Too few ideas and you'll feel you've missed an opportunity to do something better or more amazing. Some home building ideas have to be created from sources such as magazines, building websites, your imagination and other places. Potential ideas need to survive and evolve through a theoretical smashing by sceptics. The most obvious way to get good ideas is to throw the bad ones away which is easier said than done. Another issue is to try and place the genius of an idea into someone else's head. Transferring what sounds great in your head to someone else is not always easy. In setting a scene for others to build from, you need some good communication tools for your building project. I know many people use mood boards – literally boards with images pasted on Blue Peter style, ideas jotted down and even samples of materials to be used in order to convey your genius idea to another person. Then it's time for an outline plan to be drawn up. You can then present these ideas as a basis for a building plan. As Head of an IT department in a high school I had a better idea.

Forget the tiny models, hands full of glue plus the hassle of measuring tiny scale buildings until your eyes fail, I had a better idea. In this 21st century I was going to use 3D modelling software courtesy of a multi-billion pound company - Google. I had Google's 3D modelling software that I used to teach eleven year olds how to build boats and houses in a computerised world. Google SketchUp software was literally child's play and better still it matched my budget requirements by being free to download.

Once the software was downloaded I simply took an aerial image of my barn from the air using GoogleMaps. GoogleMaps back in the early days of the internet was like using space race technology. Once I had the measurements from the software I started building my three dimensional building on the computer. Genius! The software was free and I could push walls backwards and forwards, add windows and other 'clever' features all day long at the touch of a mouse.

For the novice builder 3D design software sounds great. However, if you're a seasoned builder reading this you'll probably be putting this book down and looking for something to watch on TV. But like I said before, experience is simply the name we give our mistakes. I hadn't yet learnt of 'Building Regulations' or Building 'Regs' as you the professional will know them as. I didn't yet know about what you can do, cannot do and must do as you build a new home. I'll explain Building Regulations or Building Regs, in a later chapter but I'm just setting the scene here.

Once a rough design and look of the building is drawn up an architect can be hired and real, measured out plans can be made in preparation for the all-important consent to build - the hallowed Planning Permission. The architect then tells you what you can or cannot have if you want the building;

A - to be granted planning permission,
And B - to remain standing.

If you're lucky you might have an architect as a friend or know a Building inspector you can ask for advice. If you do, you can avoid a costly service but I don't recommend replacing an architect if you want to succeed in your project. If you are really careful with money like me you'll probably want to consult with your friends before paying for hours with an architect discussing designs. Just hire the architect firm for the final design and planning application. Well informed friends are often a cheaper way to bat ideas back and forth until you need an expert to make your ideas actual work.

Generally when you tell your friends about your plans to build your own home they quickly put themselves in three main categories of response:

My favourite category is the 'Sudden & Highly Experienced Expert'. On divulging my plan to build a home, highly experienced building experts suddenly appeared from all directions. These *Sudden Experts* had a sudden wealth of construction knowledge. If you were lucky some *Sudden Experts* were backed up by home building stories but usually of strangers known only to them. Some *Sudden Experts* were even backed by a few quickly Googled facts but the most confident self-appointed building experts would appear with batteries of precision questions designed to 'help' me. Technical questions normally reserved for a degree in civil engineering were the norm to the 'Sudden & Highly Experienced Expert'. Bungled answers returned to these interrogators usually led to an assessment of the conversation towards the 'you'll never succeed' mark band of their scoring system. Every statement made in your defence after a wrong answer would never achieve a re-mark or new grade in your favour.

At the end of the scale is the 'merchant of doom', 'nothing is possible', 'don't try', or 'it will go wrong'. To give the 'merchants of doom' their credit they were often correct. They could see disasters on the horizon but given my arrogance over the doom merchants I tended to think I knew better. If you have some of these pessimists as friends you'll find yourself locked into rebelling in the opposite direction to their pessimism. You'll play a game of constantly proffering great ideas to provoke some hoped for positive comment. Ideas like incorporating solar power in your home, benefits to the environment of using recycled bricks, or use of local tradespeople were desperately offered to garner a glint of support from the 'merchants of doom'. Anything, anything to gain some support! However like the 'Dementor' characters from Harry Potter; the ultimate sucking of your soul goes hand in hand with the 'merchants of doom'. The will to continue to build must survive and you must avoid lengthy building interviews with the gloom merchants at all costs.   Quitting, thanks to these soul suckers, was not an option. Especially as I was bank rolling this adventure with loaned money and quitting mid project to sleep in an open air, incomplete home in the depths of a Lancashire winter was not a preference.

It's the final middle ground on the spectrum where most of your friends will tend to reside. It's the 'great idea but secretly couldn't care less' attitude. Any slight reaction that draws these individuals for a moment out of their deep, singular immersion in their own lives is fleeting and temporary. If I'm honest, these people were the easiest to convince of my building plans. In essence they didn't care or judge. They were content to be entertained by your grand designs and could easily wait for the results to roll in before taking a verbal sledge hammer to my plans. Surround yourself with these care-free friends because you'll need the mental break from your self-build project more often than you think.

In general, however, I was in for close scrutiny and a tough ride. With my friends I was well at the 'Sudden & Highly Experienced Experts' end of the spectrum. With humour, sharp wit and mischief at the top of the agenda these friends would be holding (and at times crushing my hand) throughout the build. My main 'Sudden & Highly Experienced Experts'' panel convened every Thursday in a pub. The friends met in a tradition dating back to when I was 17 years of age. The golden, untouchable, immovable fixture of Thirsty Thursday.

Thirsty Thursday was when 10 old school friends varying from welders to teachers to accountants and IT experts got together. A weekly opportunity to catch up, drink, share amusing stories and useful ideas in the pub. We discussed and debated many varieties of topics and ideas. Thirsty Thursday usually began sensibly but then regularly descended into friends abusing each other under the banner of 'banter' and situational jokes Jimmy Carr would approve of. The group became more expert as drinks flowed. All the while the drinking antics were encouraged by a landlord who warmed to us over the years with regular lock-ins or at least stopped watches. We could stay in the old pub for hours until other halves, taxis and trains came to take us home. Thirsty Thursday judged my progress carefully and with well-intended but not always constructive humour. To say they didn't have any ideas would not be true but to say they often didn't have many good ideas was very true. Budgeting for the expensive build by selling my possessions on eBay was one such poor idea.

To budget for your wish list the average architect recommends a set figure or cost per square metre of your home. You'll find it very difficult to get any actual number for the total building cost from anywhere. There's never a definitive number from which to hang your wish list of optional extras from. Generally a total build, cost-estimate is much lower for a new build home starting from scratch than it is shoe horning a new building from a ruin. For a barn conversion the law is you must conserve the building. A maximum of no more than twenty-one percent of the walls can be removed and rebuilt. Apparently, farmers used to convert barns for much needed money and each week a new wall fell down and was rebuilt. Eventually after all four walls had mysteriously fallen down you had a new home. By demolishing everything and starting again you 'got around' the planning law challenges of building in a field or technical term – green belt, thereby avoiding the trials of protecting the character of an old building by demolishing and not repairing old buildings.

The law soon got changed to make green belt building even more difficult. It could be worse, however, if you have a listed building you have a wish list nightmare on your hands. Even changing windows to double glazing is frowned upon. The costs of even small changes can spiral faster than the bill for wages at a premiership football team.

Costs and wish lists are hard to reconcile. You'll forever get the magic, all-encompassing and ultimately useless response of "it depends" or if dealing with an older generation "how long is a piece of string?" The latter you'll learn to wind up with a stock reply of 'twice the middle to the ends' and 'how much do you think this will cost again'? You'll also learn to get more favourable deals if you never dress well or even cleanly in front of a potential supplier. In fact, I used to add muck to my building clothes in order to look more scruffy and penniless. The latter penniless condition was not too far from the truth in the end. You should look penniless in order to get the best deals. However, remember to look good for your bank manager though. He or she wants to see a calm, responsible adult in the spending driving seat. Someone who looks like if it goes wrong there will be something to repossess or at least someone who will have a job in order to pay the monthly, crippling mortgage payments.

Being a responsible adult I was still prone to cutting corners but I reasoned that copying other's homes was a safe bet. After all, if they could build something, why couldn't I? Every great achiever is inspired by a great mentor and if a great mentor explains but a superior mentor demonstrates then it was time to find some demonstration of what was possible.

With this in mind my Dad suggested seeing a farming friend about seeing his countryside cottage and in particular his solar panels. We reasoned energy prices would always go up. So because we both cared about the environment, Dad being an organic dairy farmer and me being keen to avoid future electric bills, we went to speak to a builder and solar panel pioneer who had gone before me.

I went to visit lots of local 'experts' to learn from their lessons learnt and mishaps survived. Heating wise, log burners using renewable wood sources were fashionable in local pubs I frequented. They always had a great, woody smell and hypnotic trance-like flame effect on a room. A lot of time was spent in pubs researching fires.

Life-style magazines and the rise of TV shows such as Grand Designs started becoming my regular research homework. I diligently tuned in or read as much as I could. Ironically when I look back I realise I should have been reading journals on construction methods. But these had less pictures and my approach was less 'how do I put the home together?' and more 'what will I paint the interior like?' An approach similar to building a new car would be playing with the style of the steering wheel but showing no interest about what the steering wheel was fastened to. Nonetheless I was learning from others and once I realised from questioning everyone from lay people to architects the more I became focused on the construction side. I was learning and I was starting to grasp the scale of the project. My mind started to wander to "what happens if I can't do everything I need to do?" Doubt was starting to creep into my once confident mind.

Confidence is like a muscle. The more confidence you use the stronger it gets. Actions breed confidence and courage but over analysis and inactivity starts to breed doubt, concern and even fear. You'll start to doubt yourself as a mountain of post-it notes, ideas and 'to do' lists start to appear. My solution was to focus on the worst case scenario which I reasoned to be running out of money and living with parents in a bedroom until I was 60 or at least until I could save enough money to keep the project going. I'd probably never leave the house again other than for work, have four jobs and never be able to have friends ever again. And then I would focus on the best case scenario. A modern affordable home to house me and, potentially in the future, a family. If the project went well I would have a new home, be on the property ladder, leave home – albeit 100 metres across the fields from our farmhouse to my barn and have parties all weekend every weekend.

To create a vision of success to motivate me I thought of endless, sunny summers with my family and friends coming over for a BBQ and warm, cosy winters sitting in front of a roaring log fire. A dream doesn't become reality through magic, it takes sweat, determination and hard work to create a dream and every dreamer needs confidence. And I would need the confidence to follow my dreams even when every turn would become yet another obstacle. If you want to build your own home, I recommend a lot of determination. That's my tip to end this chapter. Dream, but be very determined as a lot of things are about to get in the way of you and your dream home.

This is a book about the human spirit as much as hindsight. Marvellous ways to buy, rent, hire, or create your way to a beautiful home are everywhere. Home owning ideas are everywhere; in the media, in magazines, to the places you visit, to the people who are in your world. Having the determination to do something is in everyone. Everyone wants to build their own home with thoughts of winter wood fires, lounging in luxury, summer BBQs etc.. The joys of house building can inspire but enthusiasm without experience is a recipe for chaos. I got anything and everything done - eventually - but bulldozing your way through life with a determination reserved only for the SAS is not always a recipe for success. Unless of course you're in the SAS. My never give in attitude got me in deep trouble with everyone from suppliers, neighbours, police, the council and many more on many occasions but also saved me in my other building escapades when dicing with accidents, explosions and fires.

The adventure of building my own home would be more challenging, comedic and unexpected than I anticipated. But enough about me waffling, let's get on with what you really came here to read about. This is the story about how my life got turned upside down.

Let's get started.

Chapter 2 – The Enthusiasm to Build

"Living is jumping off the cliff and building your wings on the way down. It's not the beauty of the building we should look at but the enthusiasm and construction of the foundation that will stand the test of time".

David Allan Coe, American Singer, Song Writer and Musician popular in the 1980s.

As a kid I always had the enthusiasm to build things. I'd play with Lego for hours and days and be quite contented to build, rebuild and rebuild. In those days TV was limited and games consoles consisted of tedious stickman games. There were two full-time TV channels growing up in the 1980s. Two other channels were part-time and to be honest Saturday TV was not worth watching. Sunday TV was akin to watching paint dry unless you wanted to watch religious shows or learn about cheese making in Kent. Shops were all closed on Sundays and Sundays were literally days of rest. You couldn't do anything.

However I did do things. I'd run off down the farm and find the biggest tree in a meadow and build a tree house. I studied which trees had the best formation of v shaped branches that I could lie wooden panels or beams of fallen branches across and build from there. The farm seemed to have an endless supply of baling twine - string to you or me - from hay bales used to feed cattle over the winter and a never ending supply of nails.

I'd spend days, especially over summer holidays, building tree houses and wandering around looking for lost, dumped or discarded items for building materials. One of my tree houses was more a series of platforms with fences around and was eventually enormous. Once I'd created a huge treehouse I'd look for more branches to build upon. Mum feared I'd fall out of the tree. She worried that I'd be left bleeding and stranded in a field miles away from watching eyes or worse still, be found dead after a long fall from my tree house den. I did inevitably fall out of trees and had to hide the limp from a concerned mum on a number of occasions.

Building was something that without reason or understanding I found enjoyable and stimulating. Not all projects went well however. I once bought a kit car and went to the local car auction to buy myself a wheel base and engine to use for the kit car. The plan was turn an old Rover Metro into something far more glamourous – an Audi TT. You can see the construction issues right away here. There were more issues than I initially planned for. It also turns out you cannot teach yourself welding in a weekend. And mechanically, you cannot repair faulty engine immobilisers with coat hanger wire and a big hammer. Nonetheless I had a go. The kit car survived my then girlfriend at the time. She said she wouldn't consider it safe enough to ride from one end of the farm to the other. My brother helpfully suggested I could make use out of the partially completed kit car by using the bonnet lid to go sledging on. My brother also suggested that the rest of the car could be used like a quad bike for him to ride down the fields to round up and collect the cows for milking. In the end the costs of getting my kit car masterpiece roadworthy meant it was cheaper to buy a real sports car than build one and the kit car was sold. I felt guilty about the sale as it was a defeat but also the car, if I admit it, was not safe. The buyer of my doomed kit car took the partially built car back to Wigan by driving it down the M6 - one of the busiest motorways in the North West.

Like most things. I was determined. I was only twenty-one when I completed the Management Training Programme at Toys R Us and began managing a number of stores up and down the country. Toys R Us taught me that working every weekend and six days per week at full throttle plus pulling off a regular number of twenty-four-hour-long-shifts for their website and stores during Christmas I was ready for a change. I enjoyed training staff and so I retrained as a teacher and accepted my first teaching post at a school where you got a salary. You also got danger money called a 'Recruitment and Retention' pay. By the time of the kit car building scheme I was twenty-four years old and just become head of a busy business studies department in a tough school. I was head of department in my first year as a steady stream of staff quit the school deciding that being threatened by teenagers on a daily basis was not a career for them. I believed I could learn and do anything. Exam results rapidly increased from just fifteen percent achieving A-C grades to one girl being in the top five of fifteen thousand pupils who took AQA Business Studies GCSE. The pass rates were deemed a major success by the school. It had gone up to forty-five percent. Paltry by my current school's standards but then we didn't have their better behaviour either.

In a tough school you became used to impossible challenges. Overcoming riots in the playground, to vandalism of your car or threats by kids to get staff in trouble. Generally in tough schools most pupils in trouble pushed carers and parents to demand jail time or the 'sack' for any staff intervening in their antics. Added to the minute by minute frustrations of broken second-hand computers in the classroom, a teacher has to develop a high pain threshold. Colleagues in my current school would be both horrified but also enthralled by what happens in these schools. Pastimes were very important for my sanity and for survival.

Mountain biking, gym and pubs were my survival route. I'd cycle from my village to the market town of Clitheroe underneath its locally famous Norman Castle. I'd hitch a lift with four other biking enthusiasts in a friend's pickup truck and head for the great outdoors. Google Maps provided the route destination and all manner of protein shakes, caffeine enthused, and vitamin added, artificial energy-making concoctions would provide us with the power.

We'd cycle at speed down places I normally wouldn't walk. We would enjoy the danger of falling and crashing around cycle routes, forests, quarries and anywhere we could take our reckless adventures. We would finish by hitching a lift back to the pub in the picturesque village of Waddington. Pub staff were always very good to us and being mates with them we'd stand well away from guests as we were normally covered head to toe in soil and mud before then cycling home to my village. Occasionally broken limbs meant a change of pace from mountain biking to walking adventures. These adventures were fun and often memorable. The last walking adventure saw us lost, huddled under a plastic map made into a shelter from the rain, eating berries and drinking water out of a stream. Consequently biking even injured usually took the main stage in our hobbies. The rustic pubs and carefully manicured gardens we passed on our rides always inspired my building ambitions. Especially when even the smallest terraced house in my village cost twice what a teacher could afford.

The gym was another place that inspired my building ambitions. The gym is where I did my best thinking. The quiet in between repetitions or 'reps' of weights allowed my mind the chance to wander. Clitheroe is also a very small place and the large gym in Clitheroe meant meeting your friends but also a wide variety of characters including tradesmen and builders. It also allowed a chance to watch some of the 'gym characters', plan mid-week bike rides and weekend drinking trips.

The gym characters amused me. From one slightly built teenager with a big mouth who wouldn't listen to advice. On a bench press the cocky teenager wouldn't listen to advice and pinned himself down across his chest with a weight well beyond his lifting ability. To the sex pest who spent each evening chatting up pretty girls jogging on the running machines. Sex pest once had an accident when he stepped off the running machine next to a pretty girl. He made the 'step off' in a cool manner without stopping the machine, went to the water fountain to fill up his bottle then re-joined his machine. He mistimed his step and was fired, missile like into the wall behind him. He wasn't hurt he said but I think he was. You then had the usual steroid abusers – 'sted heads' for short, gym dollies with the latest tight gym wear and immaculate fielded face of makeup. Then there were also the 'technique' boys with no technique, who throw weights around week after week and never get any trimmer or bigger. Then you had your mates, your own group, usually with wise cracks and a running commentary on everything going on. My friends always played hard and worked hard - that fitted my motto.

My philosophy in life was two-fold. The first was that whatever you do you should try your best. If you had tried your best then you would have no regrets – even if things went wrong. Secondly, you need five things for a good life – and yes these will be shallow – you need good family, good friends, a good job, a good home and a good wife. It was, incidentally, becoming the time in my life to put the frivolous boys' nights out to one side and find the good girl for settling down with. Romantic, nonsense, shallow, short-sighted? Yes I know life is more than this now, but I was in my twenties and this is my story so here we go.

I didn't need a girl but I wanted one. Life was great – make no mistake there! I lived in the Hotel Turner as I affectionately called my home. I lived there with my parents and my brother and life was very easy. It was great – meals and washing done. It was my childhood home and felt safe. However I had noticed one key thing – one by one the 'marines were dropping like flies'. The boys were getting paired off, settling down and getting married. No longer were days filled by work and then ringing friends to see what they knew. Things were getting serious and using my understanding of economics from my university days I knew supply and demand of the opposite sex meant I would need to settle down too.

Luckily I knew the group of mates who would help me learn a new skill. No longer chasing girls for a girlfriend, this was a new era of coupledom and a new type of girl was needed – a fiancée.

Each Saturday evening there was a routine. Meet friends in Clitheroe, head clock wise round town, have a chaser or spirit shot with each beer, chat to everyone we knew and then head down to the Theatre of Dreams (named in Manchester United's honour despite most of us being Blackburn Rovers' fans) 'KeyStones'. KeyStones would be where we'd party the night away and then crawl back followed by a trip to our favourite Indian restaurant. There we drank and ate until the early hours before taking a taxi home and having a pint of water by your bed.

Now Matt and Rob were excellent at attracting the girls. They had the banter and friendly nature girls loved, plus they had style and they knew every girl around. Being a southerner Matt sounded like a public school boy and Rob was unusual for being well over 6 foot 7"inches in height. We developed the dating criteria of the 'Three Fs' for a girl – steady, this is not that type of book. 'Three Fs' stood for 'fit', 'fun' and 'faithful'. If the girl met the criteria she was a keeper.

Finding a good girl took time and patience. If in a crowded bar we made eye contact a couple of times with a girl we would march across the bar and charm them. Ste liked his expert 'tactics'. He was a self-styled pickup artist and had read – probably many times – Neil Strauss's 'Rules of the Game'. 'Rules of The Game' basically boiled down to treating meeting and dating girls to a formulaic, computer game. A style of 'dos' and 'don'ts' to win. Generally most guys dressed and acted in the same manner – therefore no girl unless you knew something of her before could really see the difference in you compared to other blokes, unless you stood out from the crowd. Ste's favourite tactic would be to say hello to a girl in passing, compliment her on her appearance and then simply walk away. He'd leave the girl thinking of him all evening and then wait three bars later to speak to her again.   By this time he surmised she'd be longing for him to say hello again and by some weird StarWars style 'Jedi mind-trick' he was often right. Clitheroe is a small town and everyone proceeded through roughly the same bars on a schedule and so Ste would then meet the girl again. She would have had all night to think of Ste in a positive way and he rarely spent his free time alone.

So it was my turn to find the girl before home construction began. This is the shallow frothy part of the book and I apologise for the next few paragraphs but let's introduce my naïve younger self so you know why and where the later disasters pile up.

On one particular night out I was discussing the usual ponderences with my friends. Conversations of where to mountain bike to next, the bloke at the petrol station warning about card cloning and whether there was space in Clitheroe for a new gym. Talking rubbish basically and then it happened:

"Dave – it's a year since your last serious girlfriend", Ryan observed.

"I know", I replied, I could see where this line of questioning was about to go. "I've had a few casual girlfriends this year but none I've clicked with. Not met anyone interesting yet", I replied.

'Let's choose one right now. Out of these girls, who are we going to introduce you to?", suggested a mischievous Ryan.

We'd all been to the Clitheroe Beer Festival on this particular night and now with beer inspired confidence anything was possible. However it wasn't. We'd all drunk far too much and whatever we said to anyone was going to be as intelligent as squirrels storing nuts on moving cars.

"Ok, guessing we'll have a laugh. That girl there". I pointed to a couple of girls quietly minding their own business, like the calm before a storm.

"I'll say hello if you *wing fight* and take the one on the right", I challenged Ryan.

The wing fighter concept stolen from the film 'Top Gun' was well understood by the boys. The wing fighter was a friend who took 'one for the team'. As a lot of girls went out in couples, one man on his own would have to chat up two girls - unless of course his mate and wing fighter could take the conversation to the other girl and keep her entertained. The wing fighter was a modern day hero foregoing his chance of happiness in order to mentally and morally support his buddy.

I said hello or at least blurted something out that grabbed her attention. The girl I had chosen stood out from the other girls. She had long blond hair, carried style and a blue dress that flowed over her trim figure and complimented the delicate necklace around her neck. Her eyes were blue. Like very blue. The blue you would see in the sky on the best summer's day. I was stunned for a second but then the boys' *training* kicked in.

"I like your ring", and I pointed to her hand. It was not on the wedding finger so this was promising.

"You know you can tell a lot about a girl based on which finger she wears her ring. Each one represents a Greek god and your personality". I could see I had her full attention now, she probably wanted to know where this story was heading out of morbid curiosity I thought drunkenly to myself.

I continued, "If a girl wears a ring on her thumb – it's unusual and means you're rebel, you enjoy being in charge, you don't follow the herd, you're distinctive. If you wear your ring on your index finger you're a strong person. It's your pointing, dominating Aries finger".

She smiled.

Then I said, "But if a guy is lucky enough to put a ring on this finger", I pointed to her wedding finger, "Then he's making a direct connection with your heart. It's the only finger with a vein straight to your heart without branching off".

I looked at her. She was sold. Unfortunately so was my friend – Ryan's numerous shots, cocktails and homemade beer festival beers had made it through his system. A toilet trip was required. The girl told me her name was Sarah and gave me her number. I ran off apologetically to hold onto Ryan.

Ryan had fallen, drunken hero style in the urinals around the corner from the main dance floor and the girls. Our night was finished. A late night or early morning curry was required now. It was often to our local late night Indian restaurant after collecting the boys together.

By the following morning, my hangover was in full swing. I crawled out of bed just in time to see the end of the mid-morning 'Soccer Am' football show on TV.

Later that week, Sarah messaged me on Facebook and in a semi-cheeky, serious way asked when I would be calling. I had forgotten in haste of time and work pressures that I had her number. I called her. We dated. We got on really, really well and then we got engaged. I now had a good job, good family and friends and now a great girl. Next challenge – I needed a home of my own so that I wasn't raising a family in my bedroom.

Remember my daft philosophy? It was two-fold. The first was that whatever you do you should try your best. If you tried your best then you would have no regrets. Secondly, you need five things for a good life – and yes these will be shallow – you need good family, good friends, a good job, a good home and a good wife. Four out of five completed, now it was time to try my very best to get the home sorted.

Let's get started on how you get that all important, hallowed planning permission to get your ideal home built.

Chapter 3 - The Gambling Machine of Planning Consent

"Your application must be made up of:

-The necessary plans of the site
-The required supporting documentation
-The completed form
-The correct fee

If you're applying online, once you have submitted your application it will automatically be received by the relevant local planning authority. The local planning authority will not be able to process your application unless the mandatory supporting documentation has been provided."

www.planningportal.co.uk 2018

Everyone wants to live in a beautiful home with a beautiful family and complete the magazine style, rose tinted picture of life.

In reality, a study done by the University of Cambridge suggested that the average income needed to sustain the lifestyles of the average family portrayed in the Mail on Sunday newspaper is anything but average. In fact, unless you were earning as much as a large company CEO or had just inherited an estate the size of Lancashire, the lifestyles portrayed are safely beyond your reach.

However I had other ideas. A dilapidated barn left collapsing and unloved on the family farm could be the perfect short-cut to achieving the dream home. No other short-cuts to the dream home were possible. Given my tiny teacher's salary and the costs of other homes in the area, I'd financially be looking at raising a family in my bedroom at my parents' farmhouse for evermore.

The solution was simple. Get planning permission for the barn I had for free from my Dad. Register the barn in my name so that I could apply for planning permission on it. Registering the barn involved simply registering a title deed for the land at the Land Registry using a map with lines around the barn. Legally and for this inexperienced developer the map would involve the family solicitor drawing lines on a plan of the barn and a five hundred pound fee. Once I had the barn registered I'd simply fill in the planning application form then finally build an amazing home on the cheap. And cheap was the operative word. Very cheap. And also not having an emergency budget to fall back upon should have been a warning, but hindsight is a wonderful thing. The plan was then to live as Walt Disney often said – "happily ever after". I was going to be wrong about a lot of things. However, as the saying goes 'life can only be understood looking backwards but you've got to live going forwards'. That was the theory, so off I went to see the solicitor and then off to see someone who knew something or indeed anything about how to gain planning permission.

Planning permission is one of the last unexplained mysteries in the modern world. Why is one, sprawling development of hundreds of homes allowed in one field, yet next door the simple adding of a window to an existing home could be a crime so severe that the perpetrator could be dragged through the courts and fined so severely they could never afford to rent a tent, let alone survive to renovate a property ever again? And woe betide anyone who fails to complete the correct forms and achieve the correct permissions as they go about their building. Planning permission was simply a mystery and probably not helped by the media or local rumour-mongers portraying underhand tactics, scare stories of tall fines and TV shows about rogue homes going wrong.

In the UK you can get automatic planning permission for activities such as extending a drive, moving a wall, installing a conservatory etc... Big things like a new building or erecting a new garage however fall into the category of 'definitely needs planning permission'. But don't take my word for it. There are lots of sub-clauses and exemptions to the rules. For example, just changing a pebble on a 'Grade 2' Listed Building can land you in trouble whereas adding an extension the same size of your house in a terrace is fine. If you fail to read the council's planning department small print you can be prosecuted, fined and even be forced to pay to return everything back to its original state. Not a good system to break if your life savings are going into your project or worse still, the bank's financing your self-build adventure.

So off I went to see a guru in the form of a town planning firm. A planning firm well versed in the business of dispensing knowledge and planning permission witchcraft - all for a fee - of course. I was convinced once I was shown the way and shepherded by an expert that the planning application process was just a planning formality. A pen pusher would be happy and I'd start building by the weekend. If you're a seasoned builder you'll be rolling your eyes at this now. Again it's my story of an average Joe building his own home and I found increasingly that you generally don't know what knowledge you are lacking until things go wrong. And how wrong I would be.

I started with Richard Town Planning, a real planning company behind the made up name. They were based in a very pokey, small office and I wondered if this two staff band would be able to do what I needed. I also wondered if achieving planning permission was so hard and frequently demanded by customers to even warrant their services or existence at all.

The boss of Richard Town Planning was a short, smartly dressed lady with a stern demeanour. I found out that she was going through a divorce at this time and maybe I should have paid her for this knowledge instead, but that's for a later chapter. Anyway for some reason my 'genius' was not being understood. I proudly showed them my Google Sketchup software showcasing my plans for the barn in glorious three dimensions. Using the software you could create plans down to the millimetre or become 12 inches tall and walk through the model as if my laptop contained a real building. So I began to explain my model, pointing our doors, a delightful bathroom and walk-in wardrobe etc...

"Stop right there please", she instructed. "You need a professional architect to draw up outline plans. You can't do half of what you've shown me. You need to get real architectural advice. Here's a number. He'll draw up the plans and then we can meet to submit this and discuss my fees for handling your case".

I was stunned into a scalded school boy type of silence. It wasn't the feedback I had expected and I certainly didn't want someone else to do my designs. I expected an impressed audience with the words 'well done', 'I see...' or 'that's great!' I was taken aback but I tried not to show it and thanked her for her architect's number.

This was going to be either harder than I thought, or was she putting me through unnecessary expense and wasn't up to the job I had in mind? Nonetheless a quick internet search of the planning department suggested she was correct. I needed two dimensional plans. Less exciting and more boring than my work of art but I needed to play the game. It's surprising what you can't do to a building and I don't mean just physics-wise like putting floors in without support or resting steel girders on match sticks. I mean inside limits to adding extra windows, limits to designs of things such as staircases. The TV show Grand Designs had never shown people being told what to change in their plans to something less audacious. In fact, the show seemed to reward hare-brained designs and eccentric builders. Anyway, I needed an architect.

Richard Town Planning recommended a Burnley-based architect. I rang the architect as soon as I'd left the cupboard sized office with its matronly boss.

The architect said he'd come out to see me 'on site' in a fortnight's time. I agreed a time and readied my cheque book as I began to realise that the red tape of even applying for planning permission was going to be a costly adventure in itself.

Eventually and excitedly I stood in a fortnight's time next to my derelict barn and waited for the professional architect to arrive.

He arrived an hour late.

He wasn't happy. That surprised me. Unhappy to make money from me? Something is amiss here. Like a child being given sweets and yet being miserable. What's wrong with the sweets? What's wrong with the barn?

The architect mumbled a few words. I should have known or at least looked these up by now at this stage. RSJs, ecological survey, load bearing structure, vents etc... He mainly gave me a list of what I could not do in short terse sentences.

With no eye contact, statements such as "you cannot have this", "you can't have that", "you're in a greenbelt area", "you need utilities" rolled out of his mouth and all over my plans. I now knew I was heading for a difficult project but the lack of enthusiasm was unexpectedly morbid. I assumed the architect had some deadly illness or just witnessed his home burning down with irreplaceable family heirlooms going up in smoke. The mood was sombre to say the least.

Finally he spoke fully. This time at length and mainly to manage my expectations in a downward trajectory. He'd do the plans but his fee was five hundred pounds. I had looked into this fee for a simple outline plan for a planning application. Being on a tight budget I had researched this expense. My concern over adding a light and airy feel to the derelict, damp and rotting hulk of a barn went without comment or suggestion. It fell on deaf ears and looked like the architect was going to do things his way and no other way as he ignored me to concentrate on his measurements. I showed enthusiasm for his lazer measuring pen device but to no avail. He'd come back with a surveyor when I was at work. I think that meant when I was away from him and unable to slow him down as I tried to drag conversation out of him. Probably.

Back at work things were the usual business. First meeting at 7.30am, a school briefing at 8.30am, lessons until 3.05pm, IT club at lunch time and then meetings after school. Days flew by.

The architect kept to his word and then one day in the post came the plans for my home. Outline plans, scaled and measured. They were impressive as I laid out the huge A2, official and important looking drawings across the floor of our living room in the farmhouse. The family gathered around to have a look. They weren't the plans I wanted but experts said don't worry you can change these as you start actual building work. It turns out you can't change from these plans on the fly or because you feel like it without incurring the wrath of the planning department. I know because I tried but I'll explain that in a later chapter. For now all you need to know is I was ready to book an appointment with Richard Town Planning, fill in the planning application permission form and await the planning approval!

Excitedly, I went back to the cupboard that served as Richard Town Planning's offices and proudly handed the boss a copy of the architect's plans. Again in silence, maybe that's how this industry operates, she examined the detail of the architect's plans. It was time to complete the application form.

I say application form because until recently and the introduction of the government Planning Portal you literally filled in a low tech Microsoft Word document containing boxes, tables and blank spaces for your information. You need to give the obvious details such as the address of the property you wish to develop, an access statement saying how you get to the property, changes you propose to make to the property and other details so that the planning department can examine your plans and gather any information they need in order to make a referral to the council's planning officers.

Next, the planning department have guidelines that state they must send a copy of your planning application to any local residents that might be affected by your development. The residents then have four weeks to phone, email and or write a response and then the council's planning department have eight weeks to make a decision to approve, amend or reject your application.

Richard Town Planning said they would fill in the application form, send me a bill and in return I'd approve the application before they sent it to the council, pay their bill and also forward a cheque to them to cover the fee at the council for making the application. A lot of bills were heading my way but this seemed easy, or so I thought. Who would object? Why wouldn't the council not allow the conversion of a redundant, dilapidated barn into something more useful? I assumed that this would also be the last of the bills for the administrative processes of building. Just a short three months wait and I'd be building my very own home.

What could possibly go wrong? Well, it turns out that pretty much everything can go wrong.

11th March 2008 echoes in my head like the opening statement of President Roosevelt's World War Two statement about the surprise

Japanese attack recreated in the film Pearl Harbour. '11th March 2008 - a date which will live in infamy, the hopes and dreams of the United States of Dave were cruelly and intentionally destroyed by the empire of the Planning Department.'

On the morning of 11th March 2008 the post arrived and I heard my mum call upstairs towards my room to say that I had a letter from the council.

I raced downstairs and I opened the response letter from the council. The council's crest was clear and official looking on the envelope. There was only one reason why this letter was here. It was the outcome of the planning officer's decision. Excitement turned quickly to disappointment when I pulled out the by now familiar looking image of my barn's plans. This time, however, the familiar outline of the barn and text I'd studied so many times was covered in numerous places with red ink. Red ink stamped uncompromisingly and unmistakeably with the bold lettering of the word 'Refused'.

I was gutted.

The accompanying letter from the council was like a reading of David versus Goliath. A whole machinery of government had stormed into the decision process. The access road to the barn which has served for centuries as access to the barn, and its now no longer standing accompanying cottage was inadequate for modern traffic according to the Highways Agency. The barn was on farmland and therefore should never be converted to a home due to the effect on neighbouring properties and legislation to protect the greenbelt or farmland of the UK. Housing elsewhere in the Ribble Valley better meets the needs of me as an individual looking for cost-effective housing. The planning application had been comprehensively refused and any hope was lost. A sledge hammer had been taken to my hopes and dreams. Neighbours who my family had known for years had objected and even my planning consultant had given up.

The planning consultant seemed like all hope was lost. As part of a planning application you can resubmit for free an application that has been refused. Richard Town Planning gave me an option to submit. They would submit my application amended slightly again for another fee. In my head I was pessimistic for the first time. I checked how confident my trusted planning guru was. Would she do the application again, addressing people's and the council's concerns on a 'no win, no fee' basis? The answer was a firm 'no'.

Again I was gutted by the pessimistic 'no' response and all the money I'd spent on the application fee, the planning consultant's fee and the architect's fee.

It was time for a new strategy. A new set of approaches to build new optimism. I needed determination now. Nothing really worth having comes quickly and easily otherwise everyone would be doing this. I tried to remember stories of the impossible. Stories from heroic figures on historical documentaries. I tried to remember Winston Churchill's quotes when he faced the might of Russia (until they changed to our side), Japan and Nazi controlled Europe all by ourselves. I tried to remember that in the gym if you can muster some anger, you get the strength to lift more.

I was not going to give up! And like the immortal line uttered by Arnie in Terminator I would 'be back!'

Chapter 4 – Return Of The Jedi

"In a dark place we find ourselves, and a little more knowledge lights the way".

A wise, very old Yoda, from the Film 'Star Wars', 2005.

As a kid growing up I loved Star Wars. The intergalactic adventures with your best friends in tow fighting the evil Galactic Empire fronted by Darth Vader. I even had the toys and would act out scenes from the film from memory. CDs and even videos to replay the Christmas special, glitzy showings of these films didn't exist in the early 1980s. It was literally from my memory only.

Anyway 20 years later, I had a new story and a new Darth Vader in the figure of a planning official. The same planning official who refused my application. He was only doing his job but I was going to re-apply and get the planning permission I needed. I'd fight like Luke Skywalker or Han Solo versus the Death Star. I'd overcome the extensive and fearsome-looking planning application council machinery and win.

When a planning application is refused you can ask the council why it was turned down and see any letters or emails objecting to your proposed development. The names and addresses are removed from the letters and copies are given to you so you can improve your re-application or at least address some concerns.

Ironically, a little old lady who my family had known for many years was amongst the complainants. Ironic because presumably she'd emailed the council to object probably using the very computer she'd asked me to fix the previous year. Her address was still partially visible and details of her letter didn't need a Sherlock Holmes to figure out who she was. Some neighbours were less subtle. The fireworks flying and banging high in the air celebrating their victory and my loss were unmissable. It was a party from the neighbours I'd rarely seen or hardly spoken to hosted for the local neighbourhood. I wasn't invited but from rumours going around our tiny, clique village I'm pretty sure I wouldn't have enjoyed the event anyway.

It was time for a change of strategy and the appointment of a new guru. The new guru of planning applications came highly recommended. HLA were a company that one of Dad's farming friends had long sung the praises of. The friend had been a farmer and slowly over time his business had evolved away from farming to using farm machinery as a business in its own right. Jim was doing very well. He was renting bailers out to farmers baling hay for the winter, laying drainage pipes and cutting hedges across the county. A self-made man with a lot of respect from the community.

Respect from all. All, that is, apart from his nearest neighbour who took it upon himself to ask the council to move Jim's business to where, in the neighbour's opinion, it truly belonged – away from his family farm and home to a crime ridden industrial estate many miles away. Jim was beside himself with grief but HLA knew better. HLA fought for Jim and Jim stayed where he belonged. On his farm, with his equipment and his family. HLA were heroes for Jim and for me HLA were a chance to return and re-apply successfully for the life changing planning permission I needed.

HLA's owner, Andrew, was a former council planning officer. He was a tall, studious character with an encyclopaedic knowledge of planning issues and a track record of helping his clients achieve what they needed. Andrew was going to be the man. A modern office with friendly staff who took my ideas and instead of ignoring them completely, politely persuaded me to change elements.

First things first, on contacting the council for a second planning application the rules had changed again. This time I needed a new entrance to satisfy the Highways Agency and an ecological survey to look for bats.

"A bat survey", I asked.

"Yes" replied Andrew. "I'm surprised they didn't ask for it last time".

"Bats can end a building project as they are an endangered species. If the surveyors find bats or owls for that matter, nesting in your barn we can move them but you'll need expert handlers hiring and any attempt to remove them yourself to a new location is highly illegal". he continued.

I like the way Andrew thought ahead. I'd never do anything illegal but until the last sentence, the bats if any were present, were packing their little suitcases and finding a new bat cave. Now the rules were understood. It was strictly hands off to disturbing any protected wildlife but I didn't panic. As far as I knew bats and owls would not be in the barn or on the drive proposed for the barn.

The proposed way to the barn was established through another farmyard. It wouldn't be through the current right of way due to it being too narrow under today's legislation about the widths of drives and exit visibility on leaving drives. Basically the shared access was too narrow for two cars to pass each other so one car would stay in the road potentially causing collisions with other traffic. Visibility on leaving the shared drive to the street at the bottom was also blocked in one direction and not the required ninety metres in both directions. That was a straight forward argument from the council but after centuries of the farm using the shared drive it was not ideal and seemed almost like a punishment handed down on high by the council. We could, however, continue to use the drive on foot or for tasks not involving occupation of the barn. For example driving any other vehicles such as a tractor or digger was permissible but not for the barn owner's cars.

The other, alternative driveway access was through another farmyard and a long route around the farm. This next route involved five heavy duty, twelve feet wide farm gates and a sea of mud in winter. Obstacles which seemed to guard this new way to access the barn. At least strangers wouldn't be able to find us and we'd be relatively safe from intruders. They'd give up after wading through mud and swinging open one gate after another. I reasoned that these obstacles were probably a small price to pay for a countryside pad where the cheapest of housing nearby would be four times my annual salary.

The environmental survey was yet another expense. Most of the answers I could have given without expert help. Was my house likely to fall down a mine shaft? Would my front door be next to an unexploded wartime bomb? Or, would my building work cut through someone's delicate but highly explosive gas pipes? The answer to these and more was 'no' on all accounts. Was my home likely to flood? The survey said 'no' but my Dad said 'yes' and after seventy years of living on the farm the old timer was correct - as usual. We'd need big ditches for big amounts of rain but that's for a later chapter.

Meanwhile, the form filling and cheque writing continued. In the bat survey case it was in the form of the best job I had ever seen in years. At hundreds of pounds for a few hours work, I was going to be treated to a bat survey thanks to the insistence from the council. Would a bat shaped iceberg flutter its wings into my self-build project? Not if Max had anything to do with it. As we waited for the bat survey team to arrive Max was already conducting his own low-tech, cheaper approach towards surveying for bats. He stumbled around the ruin of the barn and the abandoned machinery stored under its timbers. Suddenly and predictably he found the shape of a bat. It was hiding in a corner in the top of one of the barn's trusses and roof beams.

"I'll move it on!" he shouted.

Before I could tell him how wildly illegal it was to evict bats without permits, specialist helpers etc.., Max had launched a rock in its general direction. Bang! The rock hit its target!

I stood frozen to the spot as I watched in horror. Slowly the item fell to the ground. We were in serious trouble now. Max stabbed the item with a branch and what turned out to be nothing more than an old sack to keep the wind out the rafters slowly floated across the barn's dusty floor. Unfortunately Max had also dislodged centuries-old dust and wood worm which started floating down from the rafters of the barn.

Thanks to Max it was now snowing dust. And just in time. The bat survey team arrived to see our winter wonderland.

The lead man of the bat survey opened with his first question; "You haven't been moving any bats have you lads?"

Both Max and I shook our heads as our dark hair slowly became tinged with white dust. We answered almost in unison "Nope, not us".

I welcomed our bat team to the barn. The older gent of around late fifties looked like the expert and he was joined by a trainee in her early twenties. The bat expert promptly began looking for bat droppings on the mud flooring of the barn and photographing the twisting, wood pegged, old beams for signs of bats. The trainee was beautiful and Max was in his element sharing the romantic sunset outside the barn with the tanned, slim goddess he had just met. I spoke to the bat expert, more interested in the financial damage if we found a resident bat and what it would do to my home plans. It seemed a bat could live freely here but not me. The survey continued.

Bat surveys are conducted at sunset and very early night in order to detect the little, nocturnal, furry characters. The survey team use a bat whistle to make mating calls to other bats. You can't hear the whistle so it looked like the old timer had a broken whistle and was losing the plot. The trainee used an electronic listening device to detect and record any potential replies from the bats. After an interior search of the barn we settled outside, in silence…to wait for some bats that hopefully would not arrive.

After a few hours of gazing into the sunset and listening to all manner of nocturnal wildlife coming awake with calls to each other, the expert concluded his search for bats. With baited breath I waited to hear whether I'd be spending ten thousand pounds on a bat house or bat battery whilst crying into my cement, or whether I was bat free and could continue my self-build home.

The answer finally came. There were no bats. Relief came over me. Construction could go ahead safely and I'd get a report to go with my new planning application. Another cheque cashed but hopefully what seemed like another obstacle overcome. A costly but ultimately a good afternoon in which I learnt more about bats and bat detecting.

Next was the human side of a survey. A survey to inform and persuade my local representatives for the village ward to support me. HLA said it was courtesy to speak to your local councillors about my plans rather than wait for the village planning group to have the plans sprung upon them.

By now I'd had a succession of merchants of doom, self-appointed building gurus and locals visit the barn. I was becoming quite the tour guide. I'd point out the old beams and their hand carved shapes, wooden pegs used centuries ago to hold them together and point up the hill behind the barn to the quarry where the stone slates and masonry came from. I'd point out the Roman numerals carved in the beams for when they were originally used in the construction jigsaws of wooden boats of yesteryear. Numerals carved years, and even decades, before farmers collected the wrecks and stripped the boats for beams to use in the building of farm buildings. I'd walk through the plans and the barn was almost becoming a tourist attraction as people came to see what was going on, or if my Dad in the farmyard needed somewhere to send his visitors to keep them occupied whilst he worked.

This particular time, however, I'd have two VIPs who could make a difference. I searched the town hall records and found the phone numbers of the two councillors who represented my village at the council. They were two elderly, retired people living in the village.

I first introduced myself to them slowly and nervously over the telephone. I needed to make a good impression especially if these councillors were to represent me at the local village planning committee – the committee that the all powerful county hall planning officials deferred to in their fact finding process of addressing local concerns in deciding my planning application.

I explained who I was, what I was hoping for and would they please visit. Both knew of me. Did this bode well or badly given the recent refused planning permission? Did they attend the neighbours' fireworks party celebrating the decision to refuse my application? I'd soon find out.

Doris and Albert arranged to visit the barn. Both were well dressed, with Albert in a suit and Doris in a skirt suit. They had come prepared with wellington boots and that was lucky. Just before they were due to meet I had arranged coffees, biscuits and my family were ready to receive guests but then the heavens opened. It was literally peeing on my parade. Heavily peeing! The rain and thunder began on this precious visit. The sea of mud got deeper very quickly to the point where it seemed like a 'Tough Mudder' competition just to get near the barn.

Through umbrellas and the rain, my VIPs viewed the barn before retreating to our farm house to examine the paper plans. My Dad knew everyone in the village. He had once run a milk round and everyone had seen the tractor pulling the milk float for over forty years. It had become a local newspaper article when the service stopped. The milk round and its tractor and milk float had been beaten by the supermarkets who sold milk at loss leader prices. Villagers would gather at their doors to gossip, collect milk or pay the milk bill and some of the older lonelier villagers would gossip for hours if given the chance. The supermarkets had pushed the milk round into the pages of history.

Dad knew Doris and Albert. They reminisced for most of our meeting about people they knew. Who lived where and who did what before they retired. A bond for a local boy trying to build his home had been made. I was one of them and not some 'out of towner' looking to bury vast swathes of the local countryside under housing. Doris and Albert would put a good word in for me at the local village planning committee. At last I was starting to gain friends for my self-build project. The village planning committee would meet in just two weeks' time.

Two weeks soon passed and it was time for a new event and a new challenge taking on the local village planning committee.

Every village and every local area has their own planning committee to monitor local issues and to help advise the local authority planning department. Advertisements for the local planning committee were advertised in the village post office. It was one of these village planning meetings that HLA recommended going to. So I made a note of the committee's meeting date and I went with as many supporters and family I could find to make a representation to the village planning committee.

Our particular village planning committee meets in the community centre behind the village church. The committee is made up of local volunteers, former housing officers, anyone interested in the rule of affairs and what is being built in their local area. The committee was made up of five people; with a chairman who held the meeting and four others who helped go through the agenda. The group were very welcoming and very surprised to see how many people had turned up to their meeting. It turns out that they usually only get two or three visitors at each meeting but today they had twenty of my fiancée's family and my family in a show of support to promote my self-build project.

We entered the community centre and took our seats at the planning committee meeting. An older bearded gentleman quietly handed me a copy of the agenda before resuming the discussions about different things that happened in the local neighbourhood. The committee was very matter of fact and to say nothing missed their attention was an understatement. Everything from changes in the paint colour of windows to new openings on the sides of fields and changes to people's houses were noted. It was clear, a thinner very animated gentleman spent a great deal of his time driving around visiting different parts of his neighbourhood and examining buildings on his self-appointed regular patrols. I never knew that so much care and attention was provided to make sure there's no planning permission deviance at any time or of any type in our little village.

The counsellors, Doris and Albert, had already spoken to the planning committee. We would now be article five on the agenda. I nervously listened to all the different things that were being discussed and readied myself with a script in my head of what I was going to say to persuade the committee to support me.

Finally it was my turn to speak. I began with a thank you to the committee for inviting us to speak and laid out my plans as enthusiastically and as clearly as possible. I mentioned all the benefits of recreating the barn into a home. I mentioned I was a teacher and a local employee who helped out in the family farm. I went down the sympathy route of how expensive it was living in the local area. I mentioned about the other building schemes of the larger housing providers which were going on and how mine was a drop in the ocean compared to them.

The group listened quietly and then they asked the questions. I braced myself for the inevitable onslaught. However I was surprised when they seemed genuinely interested.   They asked constructive questions and suggested ideas.

Finally they summed up my planning application. It was positive. They were going to say 'yes' if only, and this was a big if only, the Planning Authority deferred the planning application decision back to the village planning committee for a judgement. They said it happens on occasion but it's probably unlikely. They then asked if, in the meantime, we would be interested in joining any future meetings. I said I would and with that, the planning committee thanked us for our attendance and off we set for home.

We had won yet another battle and things were slowly, slowly coming together. We were covering all the bases needed to support the new planning application. I needn't have worried so much.

In worrying stakes it often turns out that many times we are our own worst enemy. If we could learn to conquer our fears, we would overcome obstacles far easier. In my head the greatest mistake to make is to give up. Nothing in the world can take the place of persistence. This Jedi was going to put in a much, much stronger planning application this time round. He was going to worry less and do more.

I was also going to find a bank to fund my dream. And I was going to be determined.

Chapter 5 – World's Biggest Credit Crunch

"A budget is telling your money where to go instead of wondering where it went. It's not your salary that makes you rich, it's just your spending habits. Beware of little expenses because small leaks will sink even the greatest of ships".

US President, Author and Entrepreneur, Benjamin Franklin.

With the support of my local community at last behind me, I felt confident enough to ask HLA to draw up the all-important planning application and submit it to the council. Again the council would give local people four weeks to register objections and give their own officials eight weeks to respond and make a decision about my planning application.

Four weeks comfortably passed by. As a veteran of the planning process I now knew to regularly visit the council offices and check all the lovely comments local residents were writing about my planning application. Normally the correspondence would be quite a weighty amount of post and require long reassuring conversations with the planning officials to persuade them that the objections were not that bad, or that I could do something about the issues raised and address any concerns my penfriends had.

Then after completing a full four weeks waiting, the project moved into waiting for the council to make a decision. This process should take eight weeks and to be honest I was surprised by how quickly they refused my last application. Speedy service for me came at a price but now the long drawn out process on this application form suggested that maybe things were going my way. In reality, my planning gurus at HLA were increasingly having to chase the planning department to obtain any response at all.

Weeks started draining into months. Months started to become the best part of a year. The year sailed on and nothing was happening. What could be happening? HLA said the service was unusual and we should have heard a planning decision by now.

I took to visiting the planning department offices during my holidays. I asked for my entitlement of a free planning meeting with a planning officer. The planning officer's diary was invariably full and on the rare occasion I could get a slot, the planning officer was unavailable on that day. I decided after a year of waiting, I was literally going to camp in the office until the planning officers met with me. Unfortunately I chose the same week the planning officer took a last minute holiday away with his family. I was stuck.

I was in limbo, I wasn't turned down and I wasn't approved to build my dream home. I was in an endless void of silence.

Luckily my party and firework friends who celebrated when I first got turned down by the planning department had been drinking in the local village pub. Rumour had it the lead club rep had been boasting that my barn would not get passed for planning whilst he was still lodging objections with the council.

It was a very unlucky boast to make. It was now summer again, over fifty weeks beyond council guidelines and even government guidelines for determining a planning application. And it was time for hay making on the farm. Once the grass was cut, dried in the sun and baled for winter feed we'd have a lot of large, view obscuring objects to store. We now needed to store the four feet tall, one tonne, black bagged bales and we had an idea. As the celebrating neighbour was next to one of our farm drives, a new storage location that offended no one we cared about was now available.

A solid drive for storing bales is essential. Tractors soon sink during winter months especially when carrying tonne bales around. To avoid this a hard standing area was needed for hundreds of the bales of hay. The grass was cut and dried over three days of summer sun and then heavy machinery came to wrap the bales in plastic bagging and then other machinery would lift and transport the bales. This year heavy machinery would be lifting these bales like giant toy blocks into a wall of bales down the rear of the neighbour's garden.

The same family who had asked to dig up part of our field so they could connect the drains under their sodden garden to industrial-sized farm drains was now stopping my planning application. But not for long.

The neighbour's wife came racing out of her house when she saw what was happening with the giant bales at the bottom of the garden.

James was a giant of a man and his son played rugby for England. James manoeuvred an even greater giant of a tractor with its bale grab, placing one bale at a time into a sturdy wall eight feet high.

The wife, Sandra, shouted "We don't care about your barn. We don't want these bales here! Take them away now!"

"We need somewhere to store the bales. Why not here?" I replied.

James continued loading the bales into place as we built our very own Berlin Wall at the bottom of the neighbour's garden.

Sandra replied "They are unsafe. A small child was crushed to death by one of these falling over last month! It was in the news!"

I had remembered this story in the press and as if by chance James had finished the wall by this time. He tested his new wall for stability. All six feet plus of his solid frame smashed into each bale to see if the bale above was safe or would topple over. Above the tractor and its huge engine I could see further down the wall one of the top most bales. The impact set it rocking precariously. I felt my heart sink as I realised that this bale could quite easily fall over and crush her greenhouse. Its tonne weight could potentially flatten Sandra too.

Sandra saw the bale lurch precariously from side to side.

"Look!" she loudly exclaimed. "The bales are not safe! It's already starting to fall over. It will fall over and hurt somebody or smash up the garden and you'll be to blame".

She was of course right at this point but I faked calmness and turned to my brother.

"Did you see anything?".

My brother shook his head. "Nope, I didn't see anything."

She realised that dealing with the Chuckle Brothers at this point was a waste of time and stormed off inside her kitchen.

James made safe the bales and we went home. I had paid yet another bill, but this time a bill I didn't mind paying. Ironically I was yet to build a single wall at the barn but this bale wall was now my very first wall of my self-build project. I had built something but not yet something made of stone and brick. I wasn't far away from real building work and the chance to build a real wall and a real building would come sooner than I anticipated.

That night, Sandra's husband came straight down to the farmhouse. We made a deal. We promised to move the bales elsewhere and probably offend another neighbour in return for the husband dropping his objections to my planning permission. I wasn't certain he'd drop his objections or what impact this would have. A few days later I gained a copy of his letter dropping his objections from the council records.

Within a fortnight I gained an all-important letter in the post. The letter came with the council's coat of arms stamped on it. Neatly folded up inside the envelope was a simple sheet of paper with a planning application number. I had stared at that number so many times on the council's website but this time next to it was an addition. An additional box saying planning permission was approved. Victory at long last! Now I would start building! I couldn't wait!

Actually I could wait. During all the delays at the planning department and objections from the neighbours the economy had suddenly lurched towards the biggest credit crunch the world had ever seen in a generation.

I went to my favourite building society - Skipton Building Society. They had stored my money ever since I was a year old and I had most of my savings with them. I had confidently booked an appointment with their financial advisor and mortgage broker. I brought with me my plans in a tidy wallet and the prerequisite two forms of ID in order to start a conversation about borrowing some money. I looked like a nerd, but a well organised nerd. The sort of nerd who a bank could trust not to drink or party away its money but instead buy bricks and cement.

I thought funding my self-build project would be an easy sell. An easy sell with such a good credit rating and long history with the building society. I'd be wrong. Far from being welcomed with open arms I was treated to a lecture on the macroeconomics of the UK. People who borrowed a hundred and ten percent mortgages where now going bust, people were losing their homes and he viewed my project as having equally dismal prospects.

"You'd have a better chance of buying an existing house. Do you want to see our standard tracker mortgages?" he enquired.

He was oblivious to my needs and whether he had targets to meet or not, I would not be giving up my dreams just yet.

Surprised and embarrassed, head slung low I collected all my plans off his table and with my fiancé following we left for a coffee shop to discuss some ideas. Basically when you feel down there is always a coffee shop that is done up in a Victorian era style with wooden floors and wingback chairs selling the cheapest but most amazing cakes. I sat there miserable whilst my fiancée tried to cheer me up.

This credit crunch is going to be dangerous I thought. Banks were withdrawing their self-build loans almost on a daily basis. Options were getting fewer and the odds were getting tougher in securing the money needed to build my home. Unfortunately this was just the tip of the iceberg. Some banks were even going bankrupt.

I visited Barclays Bank, Lloyds TSB, Santander, Halifax, Yorkshire Bank and scoured the internet for the dwindling numbers of suppliers of self-build loans. By now banks realised they were in trouble. This realisation meant that banks all pushed up their interest rates and demanded ever larger deposits for smaller loans. Interest rates and deposit amounts were rocketing for anyone desperately still wanting to build their own home. Not something ever mentioned on Grand Designs but getting money for a self-build house was like trying to squeeze money out of a Scotsman. This was going to be tough.

Luckily my mum knew my godmother had just started seeing the area manager of a major banking group. Chances like this come once upon a lifetime and we contacted my godmother to see if she could help. She did, and her new partner quickly had a member of his branch mortgage team come out to see me and my fiancée with a much hoped for lifeline of money.

When you go to sort a mortgage there is a lot of paperwork needed for the first time a mortgage is arranged. Even more form filling when you want a mortgage for something that does not exist. When you tell a bank that you want the money to secure against something that's not worth anything and clearly saw better days 200 years ago, the form filling and evidence collecting takes a steep upward spiral in volume. With a real chance of failure, the amount of money available was going to be less than hoped for. A warning sign should have been that there wasn't going to be any contingency budget on my behalf. Everything had to go right the first time every time. A tall order for a novice builder whose only cement-based project so far was a dog kennel he made for his dad when he was twelve years old. Most builders building on this scale will tell you that a building project with no errors is a story that belongs in fairy tales.

This was going to be like a game of high stakes poker with everything being bet on the property. Could a mortgage be secured in the future after the building loan had been spent? Or would I leave the bank with a valueless ruin and force the bank to conduct a repossession? If I couldn't complete the project and secure a traditional mortgage to repay the building loan I would be in trouble.

Every piece of evidence and source of reassurance I could find was needed to ensure that the bank were happy. I needed to prove that my self-build scheme was going to deliver a valuable house that a bank could secure a mortgage against. I needed to reassure the bank that they were not funding a remake of the Tom Hanks film "The Money Pit". A film where lack of experience and a plethora of misfortune coupled with opportunistic, cowboy builders not only destroy the property but ruin the couple financially and permanently.

The challenge was now to get a builder who was willing to undertake a project on such a limited budget. Luckily one of the neighbours fit the criteria. As mentioned before we had a builder who was a veteran of building projects. My family had known him for decades and we knew the council often came to rely upon the builder's firm to fix the work of other builders who had been less than professional and had damaged other people's property. He lived opposite the barn and as long as we could collect the relevant paperwork and evidence things he had built in the past, such as barn conversions, the bank would be happy to create a 'mortgage in principle'. A mortgage in principle that would be a self-build loan mortgaged to a home to be.

Collecting evidence of how good you are at building is easier than it sounds. The builder was a good builder. However signing him up for schemes such as the Federation of Master Builders just so we could build a house, pay a fee to join the Federation and stick stickers all over his van was almost more than he could take.

"Other builders will laugh at me if I display the Federation of Master Builders sticker on the side of my van. Nobody uses them. Can the bank not use another trade association instead, one that is respected within the building trade?" he grumbled.

It was a fair point but given the credit crunch there weren't many options. If I didn't do exactly what the bank told us and what some college pen pusher would say was good practice then my self-build home was going to stay a dream. A dream at best or at worst a wasteful collection of expensive papers and plans. The latter of which no doubt people in the future would remind me of or mention as a regular verbal beating around the head if I quit my own Grand Designs project now. The naysayers and voices of doom would sit smugly and remind me that they were correct all along and I was a fool for even trying.

The builder had already taken a lot of pain simply looking at costing the build. The numbers were predictably and perilously tight. The costs were right up to the maximum the bank was prepared to lend. This was going to be a build on a shoestring budget but without the shoestring.

I wasn't going to be a fool or quit. I was very certain of this but when you read this story you might disagree with me.

I collected all the pieces of paper I needed. Signed up the builder to the Federation of Master Builders on the agreement that he would not have to put any stickers anywhere. I arranged the insurance payment for the building site, evidence of mine and my fiancée's salaries, evidence of savings, copies of the builder's estimate and copies of the all-important, hallowed planning permission.

What could possibly go wrong?

Once all the documents were sent off as part of a huge bundle to the bank, I waited for the bank to get back to me.

They didn't get back to me. My branch mortgage advisor had taken a holiday, probably one of the longest holidays I've ever heard of. Which is impressive as I'm a teacher and I'm used to the annual six weeks summer holiday. On her return, my mortgage advisor seemed like the Yeti. You knew she existed because her name featured on the bank wall, however, she rarely got back in contact unless it was to acknowledge she had lost something.

The losses of paperwork were starting to cripple my hopes and dreams.

The paperwork delays were running into months. Not only were the delays about to lose the tightly timed 'acceptance in principle mortgage' but I was also losing my builder who rightly couldn't afford to sit around and wait for the bank to release some money to get started. We needed to start right away or the builder would need to leave for another job in order to pay his staff. I'd probably have to leave my mortgage hanging until he had finished another project and was ready to return. Assuming I would be able to get another mortgage in principle. Even if I forfeited the fee for the first mortgage arrangement, the chances of getting the mortgage again were looking bleak.

Time was running out. Like a gym bunny on one of those pointless static bikes where someone has removed the wheels, I was going nowhere and at full speed. The credit crunch was destroying banks but was also destroying my self-build dream too. It was crunch time in more ways than one.

Chapter 6 – Building Actually Commences!

"Building regulations are minimum standards for design, construction and alterations to virtually every building. The regulations are developed by the UK government and approved by parliament. The Building Regulations 2010 cover the construction and extension of buildings and these regulations are supported by approved documents. Approved Documents set out detailed practical guidance on compliance with the regulations. Building regulations approval is different from planning permission and you might need both for your project. You can apply to any local authority building control department or approved inspector for building regulations approval."

Adapted from www.planningportal.co.uk/info/200128/building_control, 2017.

By nature I've always been a morning person. I'd rather get to my classroom and my department very early in the morning to do my planning or meetings rather than stay late after school. By the time I've done a full day's teaching, interacted with countless pupils, managed my staff, held meetings and marked work all day I'm unfit for any work requiring any thought after six o'clock in the evening.

During your self-build project you are likely to be busy. You are going to have a lot of forms to fill in. You are going to have to order supplies and do things such as apply for permits for digging up roads up and connecting gas pipes. After work and at weekends, if you want to keep your bills down, you want to be doing as much of the work on your home as possible yourself.

I was no different. I'd get into my office at 7am to do whatever form filling was required and then from 8am I'd complete my day job. Then at the weekends I'd get up early and work on whatever labouring the builders needed. Anything time consuming or laborious, unskilled work that needed to be done was sent my way. After school I would hurry home to check on what progress had been made. You'll be very tired but you'll enjoy seeing your home come together and I was no different.

However, nothing is ever straightforward. Before you can legally build in the UK you need to have planning permission approved. Once approved, you need to create building regulation documents that explain the minimum standards you need to adhere to and the types of materials such as insulation and drainage you'll be using for your house. Yep, you've guessed correctly that this all takes money and yet another trip to the council to get them checked and approved.

Your planning consultants which often offer other design services will put the building regulations form together for you for a fee. I rang HLA who created the building regulations for my barn. They based the regulations on the council planning permission allowed plus added in the prerequisite features that are standard by law for every new building in England. Things such as air holes to prevent carbon monoxide poisoning, first floor windows that can be fully opened to allow for escape in the case of a fire and so on. You'll get used to paying for this sort of paperwork. You will then need to wait for the council to check that what you've written is correct before they sign off on it and give you official permission to begin building. Now it becomes exciting, you're now not far away from actually building. Not far from actually lifting the first of many bricks.

The building regulations were simply two sides of A2 sheets. Simple and easy to create but unluckily for me they needed the original architect plans printing off again. My former architect decided to charge me again for printing these off. Such a lovely guy. Nonetheless the building regulation forms are far more than the council simply moaning at you or patronising builders with a diagram on how to build. They are also evidence to the bank that your building will be built to high standards and worth the risk funding. That's worth the cost alone.

Organisation is now key, especially as I had plans to cut costs and avoid appointing an expensive project manager. As the saying goes and is rarely listened to; perfect planning prevents pee poor performance. I was going to be more organised than a librarian with a library. I had folders on my computer set up to store crucial information. I was organised with a diary of phone numbers and events. I had now got the hang of filling in forms so well that I had templates which I could rapidly copy and paste addresses to and from. Adding the same details such as my delivery address into each form that came along became mere button clicks. I was an unstoppable paperwork processing machine.

Spreadsheets managed my income and expenditure. Microsoft Word files held my records. I was so well organised that the multitude of frightening numbers which would later spring up daily in the expenses sides of my spreadsheet almost appeared manageable and I felt some comfort. The bills eventually became so routine that eventually the numbers appearing didn't ruin each day. I was so confident I didn't even need a project manager. And to be honest the builder did most of the thinking work. I was starting to feel quite smug about the ten percent project manager fee I'd saved. But like a passenger on a train on a Bank Holiday strike, getting to my finished home would not be so straightforward.

After an initial building honeymoon period it was back to a new and eventually normal routine. Delays started to become commonplace. Delays were so commonplace I'd gone on holiday, and by chance, this was the first day of building. However, when I text to see how the building project was going my mum said the builder had started work and all was 'great'. I was almost surprised to hear those magic words after five years of going through the planning application system. Those words when you hear them will sound amazing to you. Five years of planning have now been worth it. I felt like the difficult and almost impossible process of getting a planning application approved was in the past and I was now on *Easy Street*.

I could not have been more wrong, things were just about to get tasty, and where the neighbours were concerned the meddling I had experienced in previous years was nothing compared to what was to come.

After a week of building my Dad noticed the builder was driving around the farm lanes, through the farmyard and across the field. It was a journey much further than using the road next to my barn. My Dad went to investigate. He stopped the builder to ask why he wasn't accessing the barn up the old farm drive, using the gate between his and Mrs Interfering's home. My Dad told him he had seen the builder's team use the much longer route round through the farmyard much further down the hill and he was puzzled.

The builder had told him Mrs Interfering hadn't approved of the access.

"It doesn't matter if she's approved it or not. I'm giving you every right to go through that road to the barn" said my Dad.

Dad promised to go round and speak to Mrs Interfering about the builder. The neighbour and builder had been given our right to use the gateway and nearby road to access the barn.

Mrs Interfering had known our family for many decades. Her now long since, deceased husband used to help out on the farm driving tractors at peak busy times over the many years our families had known each other. Our family and Mrs Interfering's family had helped each other as good neighbours over the years. She'd stored the block paving for her back yard in our field to avoid damaging her drive as she had work done on her home. All was fine back in those days. Today would not be one of those golden days from the past however.

Our stocky, six foot builder was wary of her. Mrs Interfering was short at 5 feet, rotund and elderly. She was physically small in height but packed a sharp tongue and a commanding, domineering presence. Over the years, she had been known to tell the builder off for where he could and couldn't wash his vans, even if the van was well within his side of the shared track up to the barn. She even decided whether his parking spot nearby needed tidying up or not. She was also a retired lady with a wealthy existence and time on her hands.

My Dad's negotiations failed. She insisted no builders could use the drive to my home and threatened to padlock the gate to the barn. My dad prevented that. He made the gate during his time in the Young Farmers and so he lifted the big farm gate from its hinges and carried it off. There would now be no gate to padlock.

Things were progressing but not the way I anticipated.

On holiday abroad things were great however. A welcome change from busy days at work. Hours were no longer crammed either side by form filling or cost-cutting searches of eBay for deals. My friend, Lee, who I had known from university lived in Warsaw with his girlfriend. He'd pestered and pestered his friends to go and see him. So three of us set off from Manchester airport to visit Lee. Things were cheap in Warsaw. Incredibly cheap, I was in a life of luxury without the usual expense.

We'd gone for a four night visit and with Lee being a big drinker, most days were spent in the medieval, cobble stoned, taverns of the old quarters of Warsaw. Drinks often arrived for a princely sum of one pound and the most expensive cocktails landed on the table at two pounds. Lee was keen to show us around Warsaw and his girlfriend cooked tea each evening in his apartment to make us feel at home.

Warsaw was not what I expected. It was hot for a start and very little litter lay in the street. Vandalism seemed non-existent. The remnants of Russian occupation had taken their toll however. Monuments to Russia, hated by local residents, were everywhere. There were also well organised parades against Russia and the local Polish people told us how they feared the Russians returning and marching back into Poland like they had in the Ukraine and Crimea.

Being hot there were bars with outside tables and parasols open everywhere in the old heart of Warsaw. Vodka and good coffee was everywhere but being 'out-of-towners' we drank beer in huge frosted glasses and wiled away the days nicely with idle chatter.

At home not all was cordial. The weather was as welcoming as my new neighbours to be were.

Mrs Interfering had now taken to mobile road blocks that the Soviets who occupied Warsaw would have been proud of. With military precision each morning at 8am Mrs Interfering drove her car out of her garage and abandoned it across the gateway to the barn until 5.30pm. When construction finished for the day she would park her car back in her garage by the side of the drive.

The bank was also getting fidgety. Originally the plan was to build in stages. Create the foundations, then create an inner block walling to support the weight of the barn roof, then replace the roof, make the barn water tight and start the building work inside. The bank were to release the money in stages to allow each stage to be built. However now they had changed the terms and would change the terms more times again. Almost as if the challenge of building in what now looked like monsoon weather was not enough and I needed a further challenge.

The bank now insisted that an architect was appointed to examine each stage before money was released for the next stage. I've watched Grand Designs and I know not to wind up your bank manager as you'll invariable need him or her later. An architect though? The last thing I needed was additional expense. Certainly I did not need an expensive rubber stamper.

Luckily my fiancé worked with a colleague whose husband was an architect. Furthermore he knew what the game was and would do the sight-seeing visits to the barn at 'mate's rates' fees. It would require the cheque book but not destroying my tiny piggy bank. The piggy bank was already running on fumes and didn't need more leaks. Deal agreed – the bank would get an architect's report to say all was well, and that the work was being done properly. We were building an asset they could secure more money against.

On the architect's first visit to the barn building site it had rained. It had rained for weeks and weeks. On the carousel of weather, this year was a beauty for hitting new records of wetness. The barn was surrounded by a sea of mud and the architect from the city had wellington boots on and a suit plus a hard hat. The boots would be essential for a successful visit.

The new architect was a big fan of PPE - personal protection equipment. This consisted of hard hats and steel toe capped boots to name but a few items. The builder was 'old school' in that respect. He was safety conscious but more of the flavour 'forget how it looks, let's get on with it'.

The architect visited. He turned the first corner to see my Dad's friend, Jim, driving a four wheel Minotaur. A Minotaur, far from the Greek mythological beast, is a machine that looks like a digger but instead of a bucket to scoop things up it had a long extending arm that could both lift things high up or shovel things across the ground. The Minotaur was now sliding sideways through the mud, even its huge four feet tall, ridge crossed tyres couldn't grip the shifting mud. It was also churning up the electric cable supplying power to the equipment – a big 'no, no' in the safety world.

Inside the building, the builder's high visibility jackets and hard hats had been dropped in favour of woolly hats, caps and waterproof jackets. Music from the radio echoed around the stone ruins of the barn and created an atmosphere more reminiscent of the 1990s rave music scene. It didn't look good as far as first impressions were concerned.

The architect was very good. He wrote a positive report on the understanding and assurances that today's shopping list of improvements to safety were to be made quickly. For you experienced builders, you're probably rolling your eyes at this, for the novice builder here I just needed the papers signing and it was a 'Yes sir, no sir, I'll do that sir' approach that was required. Anyway, this is my story so on we go.

The bank thought I was doing too well in my humble opinion. Unfortunately the agreement that my architect would ensure a quality build and account for the money the bank lent was halted. The bank decided it wasn't having fun. To ensure I didn't have fun either, the bank wanted to make sure that the money wasn't being spent having fun, being used for flash cars or exotic holidays, they had a new demand. The new demand was along the lines of you build something, pay the bill yourself, get an architect to sign it off as completed and then we'll pay you. This was a disaster. Most bills needed me to count the zeros twice for accuracy or write small on the cheque in order to fill the number in correctly. I needed a better cash flow situation than this form filling potential for delays.

My previously unused credit card was for the first time in the history of its life going to be used. I'd applied for a credit card years ago to boost my credit rating for a car loan. I now needed to use the card to borrow money to pay bills, ease my cash flow and keep the building work going. I needed to get around the bank's stop tap and release the money to build. And then I needed to get the bank to reimburse me the money before my credit card bill started to cripple me. Little would I know at this stage that I'd need six more credit cards to bridge cash flow problems. I assumed the bank would pay any bills as they arose as we agreed at the loan application. They didn't.

Now I was a real 'contestant' from a self-build home show like Grand Designs. I had sleepless nights mulling over the rapidly increasing debts and 'what if' scenarios. I also had a new line of management from the council who could stop me at a moment's notice and even take away planning permission if he thought I'd deviated an inch from the building plan. Not a good situation to be in as unforeseen issues such as additional wall replacements for damaged walls were starting to crop up. This new manager was the building inspector.

The new form of council involvement came in the form of the powerful building inspector and this management had power. You are required by law and by planning regulations to have your building inspected at different stages throughout the construction of the building. The first inspection is to check that the foundations are correct.

The Building inspector arrived early on to check the foundations to the barn. Basically there were no foundations in the barn. A simple mud floor that needed digging out, a waterproof membrane laying and cement pouring over. I'm always one to mix things up – the floor would also contain an underfloor heating system. Basically rows and rows of piping through which hot water would flow. Apparently more heat efficient than clumped heat sources like radiators but one more thing to go wrong.

The inspector arrived and with staff in PPE gear as promised to the architect, an inspection with the builder began.

At last something that was free. The building inspector came, he saw, he went. The neighbour, Mrs Interfering, however would be less easy to appease. She'd take a whole new level of problem solving.

Chapter 7 – Problem Solving & Explosions

"I suppose it is tempting, if the only tool you have is a hammer to treat everything like a nail. Solving a situation with a known answer is like climbing a mountain with a guide book but the best way to deal with a problem you are unsure about is to think about having a break and using a different level of thinking above the one that caused the problem."

C.S. Lewis, from his novel – 'Great Divorce', 1945.

When you have an old building there are more challenges than simply starting a new build on a fresh canvas with an empty building plot of land. Problem solving and creativity is key. You're going to doubt me but you'll find lots of challenges when you're building. You'll need to sometimes step back and use the old hackneyed phrase 'think outside the box'.

One challenge after digging out the interior of the floor is how to replace the floor with concrete. A problem when the concrete mixer is 25 tonnes of steel and loaded on a heavy goods vehicle five times wider than your widest door way. The answer was not to get me to labour buckets of concrete all day. I know you're disappointed by that. The answer was to dig out the mud floor using the smallest digger I'd ever seen. I had literally seen bigger prams. Once the floor was dug out, the driver reversed the concrete wagon up to the nearest window and poured the concrete through. I know you won't believe me so I've included a photograph is after the last chapter. A quick raking with a rake and then you can smooth the cement over with a wide, straight piece of floor beam cut about three feet wide. The finished surface looked great. Or as great as bare concrete can look.

Another challenge was the overall height of the barn inside differed from end to end. As the barn was on a slope the lower side had more head room in it. The upper side meant unless you were a hobbit you were going to bang your head on low beams and the tops of door frames. The solution was to dig the floor downwards. Yes - dig downwards. Mrs Interfering had spoken by now to the council to ensure the barn did not get wider or taller. And if you remember, if you break your planning conditions you'll lose your planning permission. You will even get to pay to return the barn back to its original dilapidated state. There was no money spare to pay for this disaster so I'm guessing my imprisonment would be the alternative?

Beyond potential prison time, other challenges included how do I get utilities such as gas and electric to the barn? The barn had never had power or gas in its history and even running water was a luxury. Gas would certainly be a challenge.

Supplying gas is an interesting challenge. You need to connect your home to the nearest gas main but to do this you need to follow your gas provider's instructions very closely. In the case of gas in the North West of the UK; the forms came with a decision tree which had more flow chart arrows than a system for a NASA space launch. Once you have ticked yes and no to an endless list of questions you begin filling in the correct forms. Again for a fee. This will launch a gas connection team with the correct permits to ruin everyone's day by gaining permission to set up road works over the nearest buried gas pipe. Usually the gas pipe is buried under the road of your street and the gas company will dig up the area nearest to your home. The connection costs around three thousand pounds. You can save money by laying pipes to the edge of the road yourself but you cannot dig the road up and make the actual connection yourself. You have to select a contractor from an approved list.

The gas scenario above is similar to connecting to the National Grid for electric. Lay the industrial wiring yourself and then you need an expert to connect to the wires again under the nearest road. This costs about two thousand, five hundred pounds. This is money well spent because the stunt man who does the actual connection does not turn off the electric to people's homes. They connect the wires 'live' with only thick rubber gloves, thick rubber boots and steady nerves of steel for protection. You do have more choice with electric as to which company connects you up to the National Grid.

In fact, you can shop around for an electric connector and that's dangerous. I shopped around as I'm always keen for a bargain. A gentleman from Liverpool rolled up in a beaten up van one morning and offered to do the job. He asked how many supplies of electric I wanted. I asked him for one supply for one building. He suggested two supplies for an extra fee.

"Why two supplies?" I asked.

"Because one supply would go through your electric meter and one wouldn't mate. You'd simply have a switch hidden in your house that you flicked over for free electric bud" he brazenly answered.

His advice would be based on experience or common sense. He followed up with more illegal and brazen knowledge.

"People only got caught if the meter wasn't going round and they were only using free electric so be sure not to use your *magic* switch *all* the time boss," he stated as a matter of fact.

Simon Cowell style it was a big 'no' from me.

I instead used a reputable company as I didn't want to go to jail or the house to burn down with dodgy switches. Any electrical fires caused court appearances were going to be clearly beyond any warranty he could offer. I certainly didn't want the shock of either.

The cost of connecting to the utilities was a shock but no more than the shock that awaited the family.

Building work started early each morning. The pipes such as water, gas and electric needed to reach the barn. The pipes needed to be safe from being disturbed by normal farm or building work. They also needed to be deep enough in the earth to prevent freezing in winter. A trench would need to be dug quickly from the side of the road all the way up to the barn. It would need to be deep enough to protect the pipes from freezing over or being disturbed by anything later travelling above them. It would need hand digging or better still, a digger from Jim, a friend of my Dad. At trench digging Jim did not disappoint.

When we all woke up we found a sight to behold. My dad was furious! A trench some four feet wide and six feet deep had been gouged straight through the field behind the farmhouse, across the dirt track up to the barn and across the next field to the barn. It was unmissable. The trench was on a biblical scale and the sort of trench you'd find guarding the most secure of medieval castles. It was enormous and made its way from the barn to the road. It was unfenced for livestock or people and was an excellent hazard. The trench grew over the next few weeks. It seemed to get deeper with each heavy downpour of rain washing out more mud and rock. And the rain was heavy. Heavy, sustained amounts of rain made silt and clay flood from the trench by the tonne and out on to the road near the farm. The road was a mess and I was the culprit. My popularity in the village was falling quicker than the safety of a Manchester United fan sat in the home seats at Liverpool's Anfield stadium.

Now the mess had been made. By contrast the gas connection was much simpler in theory than the death defying electric connection needed. The gas plan was simple. The gas connection team would turn up once their headquarters said my cheque had cleared, dig the road up, connect the gas and fill in the hole once done. So simple a task that I decided to go on a school trip to a re-opened Camelot Theme Park with four hundred pupils from school.

Camelot Theme Park had struggled. It aimed to keep younger audiences entertained. Instead it was squashed between the thrill seeking, multi-million pound rides of Alton Towers in the Midlands and brash, loud, Blackpool Pleasure Beach just north up the motorway. Apparently tea cup rides and 'Puff the Magic Dragon' were no longer as popular to teenagers these days as they were when I was a kid.

Poor old Camelot needed a touch of TLC and paint. Restaurants had an absence of tender loving care and it was more the mould of an old park being brushed up and opened for one last hurrah. The good rides were gone but the crappy 'grab a soft toy' machines were not. The rides were tame at best and the pupils were easily bored but things were about to get more lively.

Just before lunch time I got a 'missed call' midride.

Once off the ride I rang back the missed caller. It was the builder. This time with nerves in his voice and the police asking questions. I scratched my head at the police presence but then it became rapidly clear. In the previous week, in Manchester a family had been killed when a gas leak wiped out their entire row of terraced houses. Today I was contemplating a similar disaster in waiting.

I'd called for the gas team many times but finally after broken promises, and the many delays over, they arrived. The gas team had dug up the road at 9am and accessed the gas pipes required. By 10am, however, their company had rung them to make them all redundant. The gas workers simply downed tools and left the gaping hole in the middle of the road with traffic cones laid out, generators still running and the smell of gas in the air. Police had cordoned the area off and were about to start evacuating residents. When asked whose fault it was they only had to follow the trench next to the road. It didn't take a genius to follow the bright purple 'I'm a gas pipeline' warning coloured piping back to my barn. I was in trouble and by the sounds of it so was the neighbourhood.

Despite collecting four hundred pupils back together for the coaches back to school I needed to act. I needed to make some quick phone calls before my freedom was over. Before the area back home exploded and before the police arrested me. I racked my brains over the permits I had applied for. Did I have all of them completed and the evidence that I'd sent these in? I was pretty sure, possibly even seventy percent sure, I had. But if I had missed any would my site building insurance cover rebuilding my neighbours' homes? I realised whilst I was on hold to the gas contractor's head office that I could be in trouble. The gas trouble was located away from the building site and in the middle of the road. I might not be covered by site building insurance. I started to sweat.

At long last my call was picked up by the gas contractor's office staff. By now I had learnt the language and negotiation skills of the building trade. I said in no uncertain terms that I was holding the gas company responsible for the impending disaster and the app on my phone was recording this call as evidence.

"Fix this immediately", I commanded.

I used key phrases to infuse some action from the other side of the phone. Phrases such as *'the police are here'*, *'danger to life'*, *'your liability'* and any other key phrases designed to elicit action from a usually carefree, unresponsive organisation.

The call must have worked. The same team made redundant in the afternoon were re-employed and back on an extra six month contract. Building trade negotiations were ruthless but it seemed that despite risking property and life the gas team were content and working again. By tea time the emergency was over and the gas contractors were no doubt toasting another successful contract renegotiation.

Negotiating around one minefield after another is key to managing suppliers and problem solving is vital to building your own home. Rarely does anything come with a manual and seldom is there a good substitute for experience. Take phone cabling. Again save money by digging your own trench, lay your own phone line and then have a BT engineer connect it up. All of course for another fee – cue the cheque book for a connection fee. Easy, right?

The phone line seemed an easy task but like all other things it was not going to go in without a fight. BT gave me a diagram of where to connect my phone line. It needed a trench four feet deep to avoid disturbances to the wire. The location they chose meant the wire would have to be laid under a hedge and to a traditional, wooden telegraph pole under which lay a junction box. Easy? Nope.

For anyone who's dug near a hedge on the side of a busy road you'll know the twin perils of falling over a root or slipping down an embankment and being run over. Or the hammering of a spade into one indestructible root after another. Carefully excavating around roots so I could hack them off with a spade or axe was painstaking. The trench took day after day like a jungle explorer in the deepest Amazonian jungle to hack through. Roots and branches fought me all the way and so did the weather. Each day started with me bucketing out the rain water which pretty much fell all day, every day. I used a pipe trick to drain the hole on many occasions. Simply suck up some of the water from the trench up a hose pipe and then put that end lower down the embankment. The suction once it gets going sucks the water out – eventually. When you hit an air pocket or the pipe develops a life of its own and comes out of the trench, you're back to drinking more ditch water as you try to re-establish the homemade pump.

It took five days of being soaked, cold and almost being run over as people gawped at the soil covered idiot in the ditch. Labouring – any jobless wonder who thinks a job is beneath him should be chained to a spade and made to dig these holes for the rest of us who have jobs to do. Finally after five days the engineer turned up to make the connection. His first question?

"What have you been doing?" He cautiously asked as he surveyed me up and down.
"Digging the trench as this sheet of paper shows. I put the trench in there for you to connect the phone wire" I replied.

"You didn't need to do that, I'm just going to connect to the new post we're putting up there nearer to your home. The old post was rotten. Did the office not tell you?"

"No" I replied, "They didn't tell me".

I could have been angry but it wasn't the engineer's fault and I didn't have the energy to complain. I slumped down and lay on the embankment in the mud. I was finished for the day.

Labouring was not for me but unfortunately a limited budget meant there was far more to come.

Chapter 8 - Superstructure & Labouring

"The Perfect Concrete:

When making concrete it's important to use the correct concrete mixing ratios to produce a strong, durable concrete mix. To make concrete there are four basic materials you need: Portland cement, sand, aggregate (stone), and water. The ratio of aggregate to sand to cement is an important factor in determining the compressive strength of the concrete mixture. A concrete mixture ratio of 1 part cement, 3 parts sand, and 3 parts aggregate will produce a concrete mix of approximately 3000 psi. Mixing water with the cement, sand, and stone will form a paste that will bind the materials together until the mix hardens. The strength properties of the concrete are inversely proportional to the water/cement ratio. Basically this means the more water you use to mix the concrete (very fluid) the weaker the concrete mix. The less water you use to mix the concrete (somewhat dry but workable) the stronger the concrete mix".

From the guide 'Everything About Concrete' at Concrete.com, 2018.

When I was a kid, my dad used to tell me that it's not all about appearances. You can't judge a book by its cover, he'd say. This is especially true of anything engineered, whether it be a car or even a home. A small car can have a big engine hidden under its bonnet. In fact, it made me smile when I was small and my dad bought a new car and promptly raced a three wheeled Reliant Robin. My dad's big new car was no match for the fibre glass, extremely lightweight vehicle and its engine. I'm sure dad would have caught him in another half a mile if the road had not slowed down for another roundabout, but the point is appearances can trick and deceive you.

In the case of the barn appearances can be really deceptive. The older, stone skin of the centuries-old barn would hide a very modern affair inside. Now the concrete foundations had been poured it was time to build the concrete block walls that would form a box inside of the original barn stone walls. The concrete blocks would take the weight of the building including the roof. The concrete blocks inside would leave the original stone walls of the barn to hide what was inside and look beautiful for a purely cosmetic reason.

Steel ties that look like coat hanger wire would be buried in the mortar courses to help keep the old stone walls and new concrete block, internal walls together. Once the new walls were put together, the new roof would be created. This would mean removing the very heavy, centuries-old, hand sawn beams and replacing them with lighter, modern rafters. On the outside of the barn, the old stone appearance would change by very little but inside the barn would be modern, have fresh electric wiring, new piping and all the fixtures and fittings that a modern home needs.

Like the Chinese proverb - the greatest journey in the world starts with a single footstep. It was time to take these footsteps - one concrete block at a time. The building up of the concrete block walls was going to be a huge task. It would also be high in labour costs despite me acting as a free labourer. In the images at the end of this book you can see me wheelbarrowing concrete blocks around. I'd wheel these heavy blocks around for days due to a unique situation.

The unique situation was thanks to my neighbour and her driveway protests. The concrete blocks would need to be brought in from a drop-off point far away from the barn due to the driveway disagreement with the neighbour. The alternative, narrow access road also meant that the huge trucks bringing the blocks would need to drop their cargo off in a wider, more accessible area. Again the nearest point was on the other side of the farm.

The concrete blocks would then need to come from the other side of the farm using the tractor and trailer. Once at the barn, a cement mixer would be needed to mix the right concentrations of cement, builder's sand and water. In addition you should add a special ingredient to make the concrete waterproof. You can get water-proofing plasticisers from most DIY shops. You add this plasticiser to the concrete to make it waterproof. It also makes it easier to trowel concrete into place. It seems to make the concrete more pliable. Another tip is to choose your sand type carefully. Believe it or not there are lots of different sand types. Builder's sand or sharp sand is a larger grain of sand and generally produces a stronger concrete finish.

During the building of the internal concrete block walls of the barn, the cement mixer was turning all day long. The builder's team worked hard to place the concrete blocks in place and I worked hard to keep the cost down by lumbering blocks and concrete to where both were best needed.

At four kilos each, each concrete block quickly became quite heavy. They became back-breaking when I carried groups of blocks across the building site through the seas of mud in an old wheelbarrow. Once dragged over by the wheelbarrow it was time to haul the blocks up the steps on the scaffolding in order to pass the blocks to where the builder's team needed them. It was back-breaking work and you definitely need gloves to prevent the rough edges of each block cutting through your hands.

You'll find that during your self-build you won't need to go to the gym anymore. In fact, you'll be a stranger to the gym pretty much all the way through your self-build project due to being without money and because you'll be bone-tired. This project was no exception. I lifted weights heavier then I had ever done in my gym past and for longer than any gym session. There's no way I could have been a builder doing this all day every day. Even with the most powerful protein shakes and the highest doses of coffee, it took huge determination to keep going. Even my clothes were giving up. Seams were quickly ripping and tears appeared everywhere. At this point you should use up all of your worst clothing presents because they will not survive long.

A hideous jumper given to me by colleagues at a previous school for a jokey Christmas present was worn until its destruction. The arms came off, the chest ripped through and finally a bolt on a scaffolding tube literally ripped the jumper off my back. To lose the back of my jumper I'd climbed wearily down some ladders and decided to jump the last few rungs of the ladder. A quick snaring of my Christmas jumper meant I was briefly left feet dangling as I was held by a wayward bolt and jumper. After a few seconds, the jumper ripped nosily and I fell just a few feet into a pond of dirty water, landing on my backside. I quickly got my backside out of the water before anyone saw me. What would normally be a sending home offence to get dry pants was ignored. I'd got very, very used to being wet and uncomfortable by now.

The ground was saturated for most of the build. I wore heavy gloves that got heavier in the rain. I also had premonitions that at some point I was going to suffer an accident so I went shopping for a hard hat and steel toe capped boots. I did have a few accidents; mainly cement blocks dropping on my head but after a few accidents and a few painful blows to my hard hat, it's surprising how quickly you learn to do stupid things less often. A small price to pay for a home I thought.

There are times when you question what lengths you will go to in order to save money. For the sake of cost cutting, hiring some useful gadgets or paying for more horsepower, it's surprising what you will do. The building of the cement block walls was straight-forward but nothing compared to removing the old wooden beams and stone roof slates. The walls were secure by now so the task of removing the large stone slates began. There's no easy way to remove stone slates but we found the best tech-free method possible. Gently remove the stone slates from the roof and carefully slide them down a gently sloping ladder over the barn's sides. Once collected at the bottom of the ladder, inspect them and carefully store the best, still whole pieces of the slate in wooden crates. If you want to save money you tend to use whatever resources you have, in this case the wooden crates which originally held the cement blocks were now repacked with stone slates. For the wealthy builders out there a cherry picker high platform on a motorised carriage would probably be the safest, easiest way – if the cherry picker could navigate the mud.

You might be wondering why we simply didn't fling the stone slates off the roof. It turns out in a building most things have a value. In this case, the stone slates were worth money to reclamation yards and to those builders who wanted to create an authentic rustic charm to their homes. I also needed to save money on the kitchen floor and on the bathroom floor by using the stone slates as flooring tiles. It turns out flooring with your roof slates is a bad idea. The stone slabs are not very good at withstanding compression. Once you have laid the stone slates, they look amazing until they start cracking under foot. Only by then will you realise you've made a big mistake and should have paid for flooring tiles like everyone else.   Anyhow, with hindsight I'm giving you the benefit of my mistake. To prepare the stone slates, power wash them off and use them for a patio by all means but don't rely on them. Use York stone for a stronger lasting finish. I'll leave this advert for York stone because this is boring and you'll be wanting to see what disaster is next to unfold.

Returning to the theme of saving money, it was decided to use ladders laid across the barn's width once the heavy stone slates had been removed. This way the heavy wooden beams could be lifted up, taken down and removed. The old beams would be replaced with something much lighter. New letter 'A' shaped frames across which rafters could be fastened to hold slates. These tough, new A-frames were much less likely to twist under the huge weight of the slates to come. The older, heaver stone had nicely twisted the building out of shape over the last decade as falling roofing had created unequal weights around the barn walls.

The old beams were carefully manhandled between three of us and gently lowered over the side of the wall of the barn and into the field below. As it was my home we were building I got the short straw. I would be traversing the bendy ladders, across the gap between the front and back walls of the barn and high up into the beams. Once the crossing was survived, it would be with brute strength that we would prise the beams off the top of the walls of the barn and slowly shuffle them across the ladders and over the side of the barn walls. Once at the wall, a quick warning shout was given, followed by a quick throw from the team and the beam would drop to the ground below.

The solution worked well and it saved money on a crane which I was really pleased about. However, I was worried about falling quite a distance – from the roof to the barn floor. With my sense of balance eroded by tiredness and only my PPE (Personal Protection Equipment) to keep me safe I did have some concerns. It was a long drop through two floors down to the mud floor beneath. The possibility of a serious breakage was high and the chance of lifting every beam safely was questionable.

Each beam was carefully co-ordinated off an older, triangular A-frame it was fastened to. Centuries of dust and the fact that the ships in those days retired their beams to local farms meant that the beams were heavy, heavy oak beams. One by one the heavy A-frames were dismantled and removed. The weight of some of these beams was phenomenal.

My arms had never lifted anything so heavy - even in the gym. For days afterwards I could feel the stiffness and ached all over. Fingers became clumsy with fatigue. I could only imagine if this is how pensioners feel when they're unable to lift simple things like cups of coffee. A variety of awkward lifting, mounting injuries and tiredness hit home.

Eventually, the new A-frames were brought into place; they were again hauled up ladders and man-handled by three of us into position. Once measured and spirit levelled, other rafters were horizontally placed across the roof A-frames and nailed into place. The massive structure of the barn roof was taking shape and starting to emerge from the top of the barn. A veritable forest of old wooden beams and rafters were now left below in the field.

The plan was to use some of the more powerful, thicker beams to create features inside the home. Features such as lintels on doorways and to use one of the mightiest beams in the best condition across the top of the fireplace as a mantelpiece.

Everything was taking shape as planned. This was a rarity for this project. But then it happened... luck ran out...

A sizable part of a beam fell down and instinctively the builder grabbed it with one hand. His grip must have been impressive because instead of letting go, his fingers held tight and his bicep muscle ripped from his shoulder to his forearm. The muscle in his arm curled up into a ball the size of your fist in his forearm. My builder was out of action and needed urgent medical attention. This accident was desperately upsetting for the builder, unnerving for his team and a warning for me as well. It was also bad news for my future plans.

Quickly we made the builder comfortable and got on the telephone to call for an ambulance. He must have been in a lot of pain but didn't show it. We surveyed his arm and I think the expressions on our faces suggested that the situation was not good. His arm was beyond a bandage and ice. It was beyond reassuring plasters and a cup of tea too. It looked like and it was - that surgery was the only remedy.

This was a disaster. Like always I never walked, I usually rushed into things and this project was no different. It was now March and I was due to get married in August to my fiancée with the plan of moving straight into our new home. I didn't want to worry my fiancée, unduly as she tended to be a worrier but unless we made it to the next stage of the building project the bank wouldn't release any more money either and then we would be out of cash.

We had so nearly completed the superstructure of the barn. Only the roof slate remained and so the barn was still open to the elements. I was about to learn the art of slate roofing. I was about to learn the *dos* and *don'ts* to avoid sliding or tobogganing off the roof on wet or loose slates.

For the time being, however, I had no master builder but I did have two of his team who would continue to work hard and try their best. It was time to tackle the roof, hopefully before the money ran out and hopefully before the bank changed any more of their rules about lending.

Chapter 9 – Getting Water Tight In A Monsoon

*"Although British Standard 5534 recommends a minimum roof slope of **20°**, some companies developed a successful slate roofing system that allows the roof's pitch to be reduced to **17.5°**. Under some circumstances, the slop can be as low as **15°** in areas considered to be 'unexposed' to the weather. This saves slates or tiles while stopping the water running under, back up and seeping into the building".*

From the British Standard number S5534, guide to roofing requirements, 2016.

Eventually the joke about the barn being euphemistically described as 'open plan' were getting old. The favourite tease for my fiancée often went along the lines of 'the good news is you have a swimming pool, but the bad news is the swimming pool is in your living room'. She was now getting tired of swimming pool jokes and storage wise, more recent building deliveries needed storing in a dry place.

It was time to deal with the vast open air aspect of our build. The roof was a considerable size and obviously ran the length of the building and again across the width. Literally thousands of new slates would need to be hauled up scaffolding around the barn walls. They would need placing in groups of ten slates at a time on the rafters across the A-frame. They needed depositing carefully. If the slates fell they would snap like chicken legs at a barbecue if handled incorrectly. Worst still, if the slates dropped they would have the same effect as a French guillotine on the heads of anyone below.

However, before you can put any slates on the roof you need to put on the breathable membrane that the slates will rest on top of. The membrane is more like plastic sheeting that sits above your rafters and allows moisture to exit through the roof of the house. The membrane avoids moisture from activities such as drying clothes or cooking from rising up through a building and condensing in your roof and then rotting your timber frames away. Builders call it a membrane because at the same time it will stop rogue elements of water entering through your roof. Without it, water can trickle under the slates or be blown in by the wind and continue the swimming pool tradition in your living room.

But hold on. Before you can even nail the breathable membrane down you need to put your insulation in. The best insulation usually comes as foil-backed foam sheets which are really easy to cut with a saw and are about an inch thick. These insulation sheets are required as part of building regulations and unless you want to freeze to death in winter or create ice lollies without using a fridge, insulation is essential. You need a lot of these sheets as well as more nails. Just as importantly you need a face mask otherwise the day after you have sawn the insulating sheets you will be breathing like a pensioner who smokes fifty cigarettes a day. Your eyes will probably have the vision of an eighty-year-old as well, so please wear goggles. Once insulation is in, you can be rest assured in any winter that you'll be nice and toasty. Add your membrane on top and now you can go for the slates. Going for the slates was the next big job.

Once the insulation and breathable roofing membrane was in place it was time for the huge task of nailing on the slates. The great British Summer Time weather fought us all the way. It rained non-stop, almost like the clouds saying 'we will soak this house one last time and refill the indoor swimming pool as a *celebratory* gift to go under your new roof'.

The builder's team were very good and put a brave face on - as well as waterproofs. The builder was back from injury, albeit one-armed, and his determination could not be faulted. It must have been a queasy sensation to return to the scene where he recently removed the old beams ready for the new roof and sustained his injury.

The A-frame beams we put in, which we then nailed rafters across, would require careful navigation. Climbing across a maze of wood would need all the bravery of a well-trained acrobat from the circus. One wrong move on the roof meant serious injury or worse. It could be very easy for you to break through the weaker rafters in between the powerful A-frames and fall two floors down to the floor below. Hopefully not enough for a deathly exit from the construction work but certainly enough to break something, including your will to carry on building.

Being mindful of the danger we started. The scaffolding was really well-built and at times I became used to it being part of the building itself. The top of the scaffolding created a great path and vantage point as it climbed the sides of the building. At the top, the boards on the scaffolding made a path around the top edges of the building. Insurance wise you need to get a professional company to establish the scaffolding otherwise you are in for serious wobbles anytime anyone moves and a litigation field day. Or worse still, you will have created a bridge that only the likes of Indiana Jones or Tomb Raider would dare to travel across. Unprofessionally laid scaffolding also offers a very real opportunity to die for your construction cause. Taking into account the heavy material loads and the large pieces of building material that could fall down, a Dave cost-cutting exercise in scaffolding was not acceptable.

The view from the scaffolding was amazing. From up high, you could survey the whole farm and see across countless other fields and farms all the way across the valley right up to the iconic Pendle Hill brooding in the distance. It always amazed me how the valley consumed so many houses and estates so well from view in between the folds of the land

and trees. It was always so picturesque from the top of the scaffolding it was hard to believe that some of the biggest urbanised sprawls of the area existed in the folds of our valley. Planning permission permitting, I would have kept the scaffolding or at least added a balcony because the views were that good. Yet, I would hardly see this amazing view. Instead, I'd be very busy, incredibly busy!

The business of keeping your roofers supplied with slates is hard. Harder than being sat on the roof dangling from the rafters with your hammer in hand. Each slate had two holes in the upper most edge of them. Two, three inch nails would be hammered into each slate starting with the slate at the lowest part of the roof and heading up to the top of the barn at the barn's ridge line. The ridge line marks the highest point of the building. Working a row at a time you head up the barn roof securing slates in overlapping rows as you go. The team could quickly hammer the slates into place and this part of the build proceeded quite quickly.

Slates have to be overlapped to stop water running in between. The slates are machined with perfect edges when first cut out of the ground, however, this is no good for roofing. Instead, a machine takes the perfect edges and roughens the edges so that water cannot slide back underneath. The best slate around is Welsh slate because it's less likely to crumble as it is weathered. Unfortunately it is also the most expensive slate at between one pound and two pound per slate. You will need a lot of slates and a rough estimation is:

The amount of slates you need per square metre (m2) depends on which slate size you're using. For example, if you're using a 20×10 slate (500mmx250mm), you will require 21 slates per m2. A 24×12 slate (600mmx300mm) demands only 13 slates per m2. These figures tend to be slightly different throughout the industry, but most roofing merchants quote along these lines:

16×8 (400mmx200mm) = 29 slates per m2

16×10 (400mmx250mm) = 27 slates per m2

18×10 (450mmx250mm) = 23 slates per m2

And just reading this you've lost interest. Anyway, the point is; if you know the surface area of your roof, you can find online calculators to give you the exact amount of slates you require to complete the job. And yes, it will be thousands.

I carried so many slates up the scaffolding and on to the roof I felt like I had the muscles of Arnold Schwarzenegger at lunch time but the arms of Mr Muscle by tea time. The combined weight of the slates I carried was huge. I started to wonder if the A-frames could support them all. I know I didn't need to worry but too much information can be dangerous. I got nervous and my fiancée coined my worries as silly 'slate worry'.

When I heard the wind howling around the roof during the barn's first winter as a home I couldn't sleep for 'slate worry'. I wondered if a slate would wriggle free and come down on me whilst I slept - like a blade from a guillotine or if the creaking A-frames would give up and their heavy load would come crashing down on me. I worried about the length of the nails used. Were the nails long enough to pin the slates permanently into place?

My advice to you is use long nails and don't worry. If things do go wrong you'll probably be sound asleep and feel little as you move into the next world. My roof is still perfect years later and my 'slate worry' has vanished. My concerns have changed. Now I'm paranoid that the tumble dryer will be left on, overheat and burn the house down or that the gas boiler will fail when I need it most.

The slating of the roof only took three days but it was one of the first and only arguments I'd have with the builder. On the second day I came back after work on a Monday night to check out how things were going. The builder's team had made great progress and I was very happy until I saw a bucket. A bucket that contained nails for the roof. It had been left out overnight which is rare for the builder. He always made a point of cleaning his tools off and keeping them safe inside a warehouse.

The nails inside the bucket had been joined by rain water and gone brown in colour. It was a sure sign that the nails had gone rusty. The builder argued that the nails were galvanised and fine but I wasn't happy. I told him I had seen poo in toilet bowls less brown than these nails. He threw the nails away and a new bucket of nails was found but it made me wonder how many of the rusty nails were used. I generally tend to forget about the incident until it comes to those windy nights where you can hear the slates lifting and dropping, lifting and dropping, lifting and dropping and you lie awake in bed thinking any minute now will I be looking up at my bedroom ceiling and seeing the stars shining through?

Once the roof is completed you'll need to seal the rows of slate edges in. You'll point up down the eaves slates which are at the ends of the barn to stop the wind getting underneath. You'll also need to bed down your ridge tiles on mortar to stop water coming in between the two sides of your roof at the top. This is quick and easy to do, but have I mentioned the weather?

The rain was pretty much continuous throughout the roofing process. The chance of slipping on the wet slates and tobogganing down the roof was high. If you were lucky you might land on the scaffolding but if you were unlucky it was a steep drop over the side of the building and to the rubble strewn, ground below. No matter how well prepared you are, a roofer's job can be very dangerous. By the end of the roofing process being in danger and being soaked to the skin was something we'd all become used to. But this was about to change.

With the new roofing in place for the first time during the long, wet months of building we were now going to be dry no matter what the weather did. Inside and dry, you could now look up and see the myriad of fresh rafters and lines of supporting A-frames. You could smell the fresh wood of the beams and I could smell victory. The weather was beaten and the roof was in place. Even the builder's arm was recovering despite working like a one-armed Lord Nelson whilst battling the barn into shape. It's funny how quickly a mood can improve when you are dry and warm. Soggy jeans dying your legs blue each day were now a thing of the past. The washing machine at home was glad but so was I. No longer putting on damp jeans day after day, I'd be dry and warm – a novel feeling after months of rain!

The roof was on and it looked impressive. Or as impressive as any roof can get. As a builder you'll come to appreciate what everyone else ignores. You'll love the flatness and consistent blue of a new slate roof. Or even fall in love with whatever roofing material you'll want to use. Walking up to the barn from the farmhouse where I lived, I'd find myself staring lovingly at the roof. There was very little inside the barn but the roof stood triumphant. Where only days ago, large gaps and holes like a Godzilla had clawed at the old roofing there now stood a good, solid, new slate roof. Now the roof was sealed, inside was next.

It was time to begin on the inside of the barn and use some of the many ideas I'd collected with my fiancé. Scrapbooks of images and building magazines that had filled my fiancé and I with inspiration for over five years were about to be put to good use. The interior work was to begin! It was also time to put the windows in to make the barn really watertight but my fiancée wouldn't let that stop a good shopping trip. It was shopping and windows were next on the building menu.

Chapter 10 – Shopping With Little Or No Budget

"A bargain ain't a bargain unless it's something you need. Men go shopping just as men go out fishing or hunting, to see how large a fish may be caught with the smallest hook. But shopping is really complicated if you are a girl, the fish are big and we want a bigger hook".

Helen Salter, Fashionista, 2016.

eBay is a genius idea. eBay made its founder a millionaire in under two years. When the founder of eBay decided he wanted to sell some of his unwanted possessions online and was so successful that the neighbours wanted to join in, an idea was born. The idea was that at the click of a button any lazy shopper or cheapskate such as myself could find anything and everything at the lowest possible price. Ebay's prices skipped traditional retailer overheads such as rent and tax to give super low prices. This online shopping centre was going to give me a cost-cutting way forward. My builder friend in Liverpool never missed a trick with eBay. Ross had managed to do up a number of flats he owned and his empire seemed entirely driven by a modest budget backed by deals on eBay. I was determined to copy his success. I was determined to get everything from electric wiring to bath tubs at the lowest possible price from around the globe.

Ebay's world was about to get a thorough searching. It was now time to get the innards of the barn sourced and purchased. Shopping for the inside of a home is not something I find interesting or even pleasurable. However shopping when there are two of us trying to make the decisions is a recipe for a good argument. The budget for this home build was tiny and due to changes at the bank most of the internal build was no longer being funded by mortgages but patched over by short-term loans. The short-term loans would be in the form of six credit cards funded by Barclays Bank and friends.

It was time to get economical on the trim and face facts. The facts were that it was lovely to have a nice interior but 'let's see it as work in progress' was the motto. We could very easily get the basic parts of the home now and then complete the remaining items over years not weeks. The 'let's see it as work in progress' was the plan but not necessarily the outcome.

The barn needed certain essentials. It was undisputed that we needed a kitchen with an oven to cook, bathroom furniture to avoid bathing in the nearest stream or a convenience that looked like it was out of the Middle Ages. We also needed a bed to sleep in and other similar homely requirements. We also needed the much talked about log burner that was to be the focal point of the home. Above the log burner would run a glass walkway joining the two halves of the barn together over its vast, wide open glass windows. The fire would illuminate and heat the main area of the barn.

However, sourcing the essentials was not as easy as anticipated. When the first shipment of paint and wiring came from Hong Kong it was generally agreed by my fiancée that I was not going to be spending pence where pounds mattered. Some items were faulty and some items simply could never have worked. I was disappointed but even I couldn't defend electric switches whose metal contact points were made of plastic. So off we set to do deals in real, actual shops.

First stop was to sort the wood burning stove. It might sound like a crazy idea to start at the wood stove before the bathrooms and the kitchen needs were addressed but the log burner needed sorting so that the chimney could be completed, and the glass windows could be inserted dust free into the openings. Besides, at times, the only thing motivating me to keep going was the thought of relaxing in front of a real fire in the depths of winter.

Real fires were seen as the best thing since the TV had been invented for homes. Living in the countryside we'd been to many agricultural shows and each show always seemed to have some eco-friendly business selling wood burners and solar panels on display. I loved the idea of solar panels purely because I liked the idea of not paying any more electric bills - ever. My dad's friend - Jim - waxed lyrical about how great solar panels were and how much money he was going to save over the years to come. I was tempted by the promise of solar panels but limited by my tiny budget. The wood stove however, was the one thing motivating us throughout the build. We had a vision of sitting inside on cold winter days relaxing next to a roaring fire and bathing in its romantic glow. The wood burning stove fire would get priority treatment. It would be the first, large, 'inside the home' purchase. The stove was expensive but small on the grand scale of things – connecting to the utilities through a trench was currently winning on the expenses side at eight thousand pounds closely followed by the new roof at seven thousand five hundred pounds.

After months of research my fiancée had seen many different wood burners by different companies. Eventually we found a local supplier who had been in business for many, many years. We calculated the size of our living room. I included the headspace of the open gap through the first floor up to the roof of the building over which the glass walkway would connect the two sides of the barn together. We knew or thought we knew that we would need a four kilowatt stove. A four kilowatt stove sounded weird because we would not be using electricity but, yes, wood stoves are actually measured in kilowatts!

I rang up the local supplier and arranged a time to visit. The fire stove supplier's office was dilapidated indeed. The run down office seemed to have all manner of wood burning stoves dotted around the dusty and box strewn floors. The office decoration was firmly family orientated and stuck, time-warped in the 1980s. Family photographs and relics of office furniture from the 80s such as plastic desks and grey, fake ceiling tiles were in abundance competed with each other for dusty spaces in the dusty rooms.

I approached the old timer who was sat at his dusty desk leafing through instruction manuals. I asked him to see the British made wood burning stoves at 4 kilowatts in size. I showed the old timer a certain design which I'd found thrust under my nose on my fiancée's mobile phone. The tip I want to give you here is that British steel made, wood burning stoves tend to have less sulphur content in the steel than the popular, much cheaper Chinese designs. A friend had a Chinese stove that lasted just four years before a large crack opened up and rendered it useless. As a result stoves made from British steel are less likely to crack under heat and I thought given my luck in the coldest winter I could see my wood burning stove breaking in half if I pulled my cheapskate routine here.

The old timer showed us a few different stoves. He explained the price differences. Whilst my fiancée kept him occupied with a range of features and colour questions I quickly Googled the models to see if I was getting a great deal. The old timer knew everything about wood burning stoves and being convinced of his expertise and product quality I paid a deposit ready for the delivery. Stove sorted for now, it was time to shop for bathroom furniture next.

The task was to find bathroom furniture cheaply. The builder had an ace up his sleeve in the form of a builder's only bathroom merchant. It was an ace as the merchant was supplying high quality Burlington bathroom pieces - toilets, baths and sinks in the old English style my fiancée dreamed about. With my fiancée we had done the traditional shopping routine of visiting everywhere, speaking to every earnest, sincere but ultimately pushy bathroom sales person we could find. Even in supposed bathroom warehouse type of businesses with rock bottom prices we were struggling on our budget.

Finally, using the builder's contact, we went wholesale and achieved an eye-watering massive fifty to sixty percent off the prices other retailers had shown us for the very same bathroom set. We had spent hours trawling the internet and visiting anyone and everyone who sold bathrooms. The builder had a better idea. He recommended a trade only bathroom dealer and I should go as one of his members of staff. This would be a genius move.

I went with my fiancée to visit the builder's recommended supplier. The supplier was based in what looked like an old car garage. It was run down and appearance wise it did not look promising. Weeds grew out of the car park wall and broken glass cracked under foot. The supplier's building needed a new coat of paint and a good scrubbing of the blacked out windows.

However, you should never judge a book by its cover and this supplier was one of those books. Inside the building there were mocked up exhibitions of a huge number of bathrooms. The inside was an Aladdin's cave of bathroom items and accessories. And it was cheap. Very cheap. The same items frustratingly just beyond the reach of our budget were now back, lovingly displayed and alluringly within our budget.

My fiancée could safely have all of the bathroom pieces she wanted. I was so overjoyed when I visited the builder's choice of supplier I almost went out to the nearest pub to celebrate. Far from being a negotiating genius I turned into an amateur gibbering wreck. I couldn't stop myself from constantly questioning and asking the salesman if the prices were correct, if the VAT had somehow been missed off and what the catch was. I was like a patient getting the 'all clear' from the doctor for some serious illness or a desperate gambler down to his last tenner coming up with a life-saving win.

Buoyed up by this massive success, the following weekend we headed out in the car to look for kitchen manufacturers and wholesalers. The kitchen would be the last of the big expensive, interior parts of the house other than the glass balustraded walkway. I was confident that we'd get another great deal now we knew what to look for and where. However bad luck was about to catch up with us.

Kitchens are a massively over complicated item. They are sold using 3D modelling software using technology that could design space rockets. A potential kitchen comes with an enormous amount of variation in colours, features, storage, styles, equipment etc.., you get the picture. For a place to simply eat and cook your food there was a massive amount of sharks and horror tales for would-be buyers as they flapped around in the pool of kitchen sharks.

One kitchen supplier had even heard of my barn development from the council's planning department website. The council website listed all approved local planning permissions and the kitchen supplier offered to sell us a bespoke kitchen. It turns out all kitchens are tailored, bespoke to the dimensions of a home no matter who supplies them. He wanted a mere forty thousand pounds for one of his kitchens! I joked I could build an extension for that price but he still left me magazines each week and voicemails. I have no idea where he got my mobile phone number from but his brazen, determined attitude suggested that data protection legislation was not something that was going to trouble him in his persistent quest for sales. His price, however, was another issue.

The pricing points of kitchens are a work of malevolent genius in themselves. You can spend a little and end up with a kitchen Fred

Flintstone had built or you could use up an entire mortgage just on the kitchen alone. A ballpark figure seemed to be five thousand pounds for a small kitchen and 'the sky's the limit' for a bigger kitchen. The amount of compromises you need to make to keep your budget on track will gain quite a lot of stern looks, tittering and belittling. That's the general response from sales reps looking to extort every last penny out of you despite your willingness to spend thousands in the first place. They prey on weakness or chinks in your armour. I had a chink in my armour and our kitchen saleswoman was about to talk kitchens.

The talk was about to begin. After months of searching and what felt like weeks of reading, my fiancée had set her heart on a particular kitchen she had seen in the posh, and in my opinion, ridiculously expensive lifestyle pages of the local 'Live Valley' magazine.

The magazine was free in certain postcode areas - usually free ironically - for the wealthier postcodes where most properties had garages bigger than most people's homes, and paying for a magazine was more an inconvenience than a luxury. Once set on a particular designer she had seen in the magazine, the inevitable visit to their offices and showroom was next.

Ordering a kitchen was the easy part, it was quite another task to get the kitchen designed. It literally took weeks and weeks once we had found the kitchen designer and supplier. What I could not understand was how simple measurements from the barn's kitchen size to ceiling heights were complicated into a myriad of other issues which generally meant a price rise for them and a dent in the budget for me.

Details about floor levels, venting fumes out of the kitchen, the appliance order and ergonomics plus other details soon rapidly piled into the designer's mix. Just trying to keep up with the daily email correspondence for the kitchen alone was a job in itself. The kitchen was eventually designed and approved by my fiancée. She was very excited to be gaining a kitchen straight out of a magazine. I was just hoping we could get it to fit together and make the kitchen look like the example in the magazine. It would take a few weeks for the factory to turn plans into actual parts. Once machined, the kitchen would be delivered to us for assembly on site.

Unfortunately we would later find that the arrival of the kitchen furniture would equally be a convoluted circus of missing parts, follow up phone calls and a disaster. The delivery was a process not too far from those magazines you used to collect as a kid, where you built a model airplane one piece at a time per magazine edition over a period of months, if not years.

The kitchen wasn't on its own for causing headaches. A simple task such as putting a credit card through a card reader and giving an address always seems to be the easiest part of buying large items for the barn. For example, the glass walkway which would join the two halves of the barn over the top of the huge windows was one such challenge. The bridge if you will, between the taller part of the barn to the shallower half of the barn would be a three metre walkway underpinned by dressed steel girders. The walkway would be flanked by Grand Designs style sheets of glass to form the railings so you didn't fall from the first floor to the ground floor. Again, this was going to arrive airplane kit magazine style over a period of weeks rather than all at once.

But for now I had a greater challenge. Windows for each of the barn's openings had arrived. It was time to put the windows in, in order to seal up the last entry points and to prevent water from creating a paddling pool on the ground floor.

The windows were double glazed and slightly tinted. In the battle with the planning department all rights to create new window openings had been taken away. Also in a frustrating decision, the council insisted not on maintenance-free wood appearance plastic windows but on wood framed windows on the grounds of authenticity with the local neighbourhood. I looked at everyone's windows. An older lady had crumbling wood framed windows, everyone else had joined the modern age of plastic frames. Just in case I tried to pull a 'fast one', copies of the window frame material would need to be sent to the council to prove that I was using as much as possible local stone for lintels over windows and wood to hold the glass window panes in place. Wood frames would be made for each window. The wood beading would sandwich the glass in place and each window would be delivered as custom cut glass sheets. Then as a complete unit, the wood frames would be used alongside concrete to hold the window glass in place.

The windows were carefully dropped off by the glass company and had been stored in one of the farm's buildings for later use on my barn. It was now time to bring out the industrial saw machine. We would cut strips of window frames and begin cutting wood beading in order to fit the glass windows into their positions on the barn. The wood window frames would give a bit of leeway when dealing with a barn where not one wall or opening was completely straight due to farmers' limited building skills two hundred years ago.

The most impressive windows were the two metre tall, three metre wide openings located on opposite sides of the barn in the middle of the long sides of the building. These vast pieces of glass covered the old entrances that horse and cart and later tractor and trailers would have entered the building by. We were not allowed any new openings in order to preserve the barn's character so these big windows would also be the biggest source of light in the barn. The glass walkway mentioned previously wasn't decadent but an attempt to join the barn together without blocking the valuable natural light and racking up grey skin and artificial lighting bills in the years to come.

Painstakingly, superb craftsmanship was required to complete the carpentry needed to keep the windows in place. The windows were slightly tinted to avoid glare inside the barn and to avoid cooking everyone inside the barn in the summer months. The wood would also flex as temperatures changed outside.

The windows were a significant milestone. The building was now waterproof and ready for its internal features. More importantly, we had achieved on a shoestring and credit card budget another stage of the build. Now I could get my architect back and, with a successful report from the architect, go 'cap in hand' back to the bank to beg for the next release of money to pay my bills. And the bills were big.

The majority of the bills weren't in what I would call the 'additional extras' category of expenditure for the barn but for the 'essentials we cannot do without' zone. It was impossible not to invest in having a roof, floors, walls and the watertight environment that no longer needed wellington boots when inside the home. The bill in the region of fifty thousand pounds was coming, not a lot considering how much had been done to convert the building into one that now very closely resembled a home.

The architect came back. He was impressed by what had been done and readily signed off the work so far for the bank. For a small fee for the report of course. I'd have a lot of architect reports and fees by the end. Now I simply needed to chase my branch mortgage manager to release the next funds. We'd need the next release of funds before the builder and his team got wind of how little money I had to pay the crippling bills which were starting to mount up.

But for now I could celebrate. I now had a watertight shell of a building and the contents were going to be arriving very soon. It was time for a quick beer. A quick beer because by now I was so tired from school work and building that any booze whatsoever sent me straight to sleep. But I had a barn for a home, with the interior on order and I slept well that night. I knew fresh money was coming to help me continue my home.

The next stage would be to start the interior fittings of the barn and confidence of hitting this building milestone was high.

Chapter 11 – The Neighbour Wants Building Work Halting

"Culture makes people understand each other better. And if they understand each other better in their soul, it is easier to overcome the economic and political barriers. But first they have to understand that their neighbour is, in the end, just like them, with the same problems, the same questions. We make our friends; we make our enemies; but God makes our next door neighbour".

Paulo Coelho, Brazilian Novelist, 2016.

Mrs Interfering wasn't happy. She wasn't any one of the other dwarfs either that Snow White had the chance to meet. Trouble was brewing in the heart of Mrs Interfering. She always referred to the barn as 'her barn'. Over the years if a cow went into labour on the farm she might ring up and say it's near 'her barn', or if a wily sheep escaped she might say it broke out through a fence near 'her barn'.

The only problem was as Mrs Interfering was getting older I generally began to think she believed the barn was hers or at least she wanted it for her younger son who she suggested would be a perfect tenant for the barn. Anyhow, speculation over, Mrs Interfering was causing more than her usual roadblock problems. This time she was threatening legal action to anyone seen walking up the shared drive or, heaven forbid, leaving a works van at my end of the shared access.

Delivery staff trying to do their jobs were filmed by Mrs Interfering with a determination reserved only for the CCTV staff at a bank or watching employees with money at a casino. Notes were made and notes started to find their way from Mrs Interfering to the council despite the council acknowledging our every right to use the access. My fiancée's elderly father was shaken up by the old coffin dodger ranting at him on his way to see the barn. Not a reassuring first impression of where his youngest daughter would be living in a few months' time. Neither her age nor dignity were going to stop Mrs Interfering from asserting her own view on us.

Mrs Interfering had a fiery temper and was not one for enjoying change. Idle legal threats to any visitor to the barn whether it be suppliers dropping off materials or my fiancée's family visiting at the drive were starting to be backed up by letters from her solicitor. Polite negotiation in person with Mrs Interfering was falling on deaf ears and it was clear a new expense was coming my way. I would be needing legal insurance and a legal penfriend to write back to Mrs Interfering.

I spoke to our family solicitor. His expression said it all. He was not surprised that the building was causing upset with the neighbours. Despite my attempts to route the overwhelming majority of traffic through the farm and not the nearest shared driveway Mrs Interfering was enraged. The route was kept clean and tidy but to no avail. Noise was non-existent before the morning cup of breakfast tea and things were silent after staff had exited for tea time. In fact the low tech, cost-cutting consciousness of the build meant little heavy plant equipment was used and peace shattering noise rarely ever emanated from my building site. The problem my solicitor stated was clear;

"You live, David, in a relatively wealthy area with a lot of bored retirees who have a lot of time and money on their hands. People don't like change and you are there, young and making a change", he asserted.

"What do I do then?" I enquired.

"We'll send a letter to calm things down and gently assert you rights not to have your access blocked or your visitors interfered with. We don't want to spend money in a 'tit for tat' correspondence but we'll see what happens", he replied.

On the way home I mulled over what my solicitor had said. I could sense a new building experience and expense was heading my way.

I spoke to Ross in Liverpool and he recommended taking insurance out to avoid the costly iceberg of dealing with my solicitor loving penfriend. I spoke to the bank and it turns out you can get legal insurance for very little. For roughly £50 a year Barclays Bank will insure you with your existing building insurance for unlimited calls to a solicitor for legal advice. If things escalated further to affect the enjoyment of your home or threatened the access to your home then you have your own legal team. This was going to get useful and even essential in future. At the moment Mrs Interfering was just a nuisance however this would soon change when her sons got involved.

Mrs Interfering's claims were becoming more extreme. The builder lived next to my barn and across a driveway from Mrs Interfering. She even suggested that part of the builder's land was actually hers. When challenged about the claim and the fact that the land was clearly on the builder's deeds she stated the land was also on her deeds. This was an impossibility and should you find yourself at the mercy of a neighbour who claims your land you need to head to the Land Registry. Deeds of your land and your neighbour's land, or in fact anyone's land, can be downloaded from the government keeper of land records for twenty pounds per set. She also alleged that part of my property was also hers. Again the title deeds for my land and garage were clear but the stress and horror stories from shows like 'Nightmare Neighbours From Hell' and stories in the press of neighbours parting with vast sums of money because someone had done something simple like placing a plant pot in the wrong place were common.

Mrs Interfering was starting to frighten me. She was becoming obsessive. She took to standing in the window of her home whenever I was working outside on a weekend. Most dangerously, she also began to take a very keen interest in how my home was being built and this was going to start to cost money. She hired a professional architect and building company. This company was going to monitor my every move and even the smallest discrepancy was being relayed to the council planning department. I can only imagine what the council officer on the receiving end of a daily commentary on my work was thinking. Personally I'd use the right mouse button and select the spam option for Mrs Interfering's correspondence. Unfortunately, a spam setting might send her messages directly to the electronic dustbin of the planning department's email system but the planning enforcement officer was duty bound to investigate all and any complaints made.

A two-hundred-year-old-wall in the garden had to be demolished because my architect hadn't drawn a line on the map to say it should stay. Simple errors that neither I, the council nor the builder would notice were now going to the council. The council were then duty-bound to investigate. Things like the drive through the farm being too wide or the farm's wire fencing that criss-crossed most farms saving money and effort to build were to be replaced. And replaced by expensive, view masking, dry stone walls – all because of tiny administrative errors. I'd concentrated on building my home on a limited budget with the view to fixing the places where I would not be sleeping at a later date. An error looking back but it was too late.

It was time to install the paranoid man's dream – CCTV. The barn was now watertight and I bought the latest Swann security system with four cameras and a hard drive containing a box which powered the cameras and stored their data. It sounds expensive but 'all in', it was two hundred and fifty pounds. This was the price I was willing to pay to protect my new home and defend myself in court should Mrs Interfering's accusations get worse. And they did get worse. The first movement detected by the cameras after work had finished for the day was the dreaded Council Building Enforcement Officer. He was on video, complete with official looking clipboard, suit and escorted by a less than neutral son of Mrs Interfering. The Council Building Enforcement Officer arrived a number of times.

Enter the self-builder's nightmare – the Building Enforcement officer. In the building world these officers are backed with the powers of God. If they are reasonable you get chance to put your 'misdemeanours' right. If you're unlucky you get a life crippling fine or if you really upset God's minions you get to pay to return the property back to its original state. The latter in my case, as I had got so far, would be a cost in the tens of thousands of pounds. I would eventually see five of these Building Enforcement Officers over the build of my home, all for separate reasons, and all at the beck and call of my lovely neighbours.

The first Building Enforcement Officer visit was with Mrs Interfering's son. The son had also taken an interest in my barn building despite living a good number of miles away. Mrs Interfering's son pointed out and photographed along with the inspector everything he felt was wrong with my building. For a good ten minutes I watched the CCTV recording of the visit, unable to answer the Enforcement Officer's questions and unsure of what I was going to be guilty of. I had to wait a very long two weeks until I found out what had been discussed. I began to hope that the officer had believed there was 'no case' to answer like in a court room TV show I'd seen recently and would never write to me.

My fears came true however. A Ribble Valley Borough Council crested envelope soon dropped through the farm house letter box and with it the stern allegations written in a legal speak of 'point 10 refers to planning application dated 20th April 2012 and states..' and 'Ribble Valley policy point ten, subsection four states that you have contravened....'.

I don't remember the actual numbers but you get the gist. The threats all came with a prosecution warning. I was in trouble. It was again time to pay more money and ask my heroes at HLA to speak to the council and negotiate a truce.

After a few sleepless nights the response HLA had from the planning enforcement officer was in. After the building was complete I had to demolish the path to the shared access and that unless I was on foot I was no longer welcome to use the shared drive to access the barn. A wall would have to be built before first occupying the barn in order to prevent use of the shared access.

This was devastating and exactly what Mrs Interfering wanted – a blanket ban on me using the drive and to divert precious money to building the alternative driveway quickly. The stone wall to mark the edge of my curtilage would cut off access to my garage located further down the shared access and stop centuries old access by the farm through that route. It would be another planning application to vary the planning conditions. Again another cost and another pre-work routine of form filling and collecting of supporting evidence with no guarantee of success. Mrs Interfering was stamping all over my dream home. She was coldly and maliciously ruining my home.

But that wasn't enough, Mrs Interfering was on the offensive. Mrs Interfering was not happy enough with the planning costs imposed or the cost of changing drives or anything else. She was instead onto her next stage of mayhem – calling the police. My fiancée was a quiet living girl in a strange part of the world and as we are both teachers, we are regularly checked to ensure we are suitable to teach children each year so our involvement with the police was not the sort of activity that would:

A, help us keep our jobs.

And B, impress the head teacher if the allegations on our criminal record meant a check came back as 'failed'.

The first police officers, and there would be more – 26 different officers in fact and that is not counting repeat visitors, were initially very helpful. They were of the opinion that if no one blocks the shared access or speaks to the other 'party' everything would be fine. Accusations ranged from us blocking Mrs Interfering in, to blocking her from blocking our visitors in and her blocking our gate. It was all about 'blocking'. It was petty but being unfamiliar to police involvement except for my younger days spent watching episodes of the police show 'The Bill', the intervention of police officers made my heart rate jump. The police involvement was helpful but Mrs Interfering would ramp up the pressure to ensure I didn't get comfortable with their involvement.

Eventually, I would realise that the situation was not yet at the top of the mountain and we still had to descend into the chaos and arrests that were to follow.

There was one side effect of the nuisance. I was maturing. I was learning at a geometric rate about things such as planning law, dealing with solicitors and standing up to excessively demanding neighbours. Years ago, I wouldn't say boo to a goose. With strangers now turning up for Mrs Interfering and the heavier, physical side of the build project diminishing I was hitting the gym more regularly. I was mentally and physically much stronger and the later in-your-face arguments with Mrs Interfering's boys that would have frightened me as a young twenty something no longer intimidated me. If they wanted to threaten me it was becoming too late. Being stressed to a point of no return I'd developed mental and physical armour plating a battleship would be proud of.

Anyway I had more practical things to think about. Unless I was going to shower in a passing stream or cook food over a candle I was going to have to sort out the utilities of the barn. I needed mod cons of bathrooms with water, lights powered by electric and gas heating. It was time to bring the centuries-old barn into the modern age!

Chapter 12 – The Age of Utilities!

"Electrical installation work is governed by industrial standards and a legal framework. The most significant example of standards is the British Standard 7671 which is referred to directly by the Electricity at Work Act (1989) and is in Part P of the Building Regulations. The laws of what you can do or cannot do are also enshrined in the Building Act 1984 & 2000 which provide the Building Regulations which exist to promote standards for most aspects of a building's construction, its structure, and safety such as electrics".

Adapted from NICENIC.com, 2018.

Simple things in life often provide the greatest satisfaction. There is no greater truth than this in your self-build project. Simple joys such as turning a tap on and water comes out, or the fact your boiler can produce hot water. Or even being able to switch a light on without stumbling around looking for a torch or a match as the sun goes down. Simple pleasures that will make you happier than the average person will ever know.

Believe it or not, you - the novice - can install some of the electrics in your home yourself despite the stories about how difficult it is to find a good, qualified electrician and the complexity of wiring. But before you follow me into a cost-cutting exercise and hire an electrician for only the most serious electrical jobs, stop and think. You need an Electrical Compliance Certificate for your building insurer in order to prove your home will not burn down or at least it won't burn down due to anything you've done to the electrics. You are also tampering with the only force that beyond a heavy digger, gas explosion or some sort of powerful power tool that can end your life in under a second. Pretty heavy eh? But don't worry, electrics done well will be fine and you'll forget all about them in time as they lie quietly buried under your plasterboard.

The big thing about electrics is planning where each circuit or loop will power what area of your home. Larger power supplies are needed for heavy circuits such as the one the kitchen oven will reside on. Smaller currents will go through things such as lighting and your burglar alarm. You'll plan the cables in detail but forget this for a moment. The main thing to think of is how you will use your home. Where will the TV be? Will there be enough sockets to power your TV, games console and Sky or Freeview box wherever the TV will be? Remember for light switches you need the switch handy before you enter and exit each room or you'll be fumbling in the dark like a love struck teenager for most of the darker, winter months. Similarly, unless you want to use battery powered vacuum cleaners with all the power of an asthmatic sucking through a straw; you need to put plug sockets at the top and bottom of stairwells. You'll also need extra sockets for all your kitchen gadgets. And sockets plus aerial connection for the TV in the kitchen if you're posh. Once you've done all this thinking, photograph your wiring like an archaeologist photographs a tomb or you'll be putting nails and your life on the line for years to come. Label up your circuits in the fuse box (also known as your consumer unit) carefully or you'll find switching a circuit off for a particular room can be like a puzzle from the TV programme 'Crystal Maze'.

I didn't have this advice at the beginning of my build. Now cables which should only go horizontally or vertically, attached to the studs or wooden posts behind your plasterboard could go diagonally or even round and round in circles. Just mounting a TV to the kitchen wall had me sweating recently. I wondered whether each turn of the screws designed to mount the TV to the wall were taking me closer to my own electrocution or whether I would live to see the night's episode of Coronation Street.

Wiring once put into place needs testing thoroughly and only an electrician should be doing this testing work. It might also be an idea to ask your sparkie – the industry cool term for an electrician – if he or she could put in your phone lines. BT will connect to the outside of your property for two hundred pounds. Once they have positioned a live telephone line outside your home you must take this master telephone line into your property. Then you divide it up between each additional phone socket you want around the home. Get it right and you'll be able to ring friends. Get it wrong and you'll have broadband speeds below the bandwidth of early dial up modems. The BT fault finding engineer proudly found the latter scenario in my home and now I only have broadband on my mobile phone.

Water and heating is similar to electric. Some parts such as bending the heating pipes through holes from room to room can be done by yours truly. However fitting a gas boiler yourself can significantly ruin your house and make it unintentionally open plan. Only an expert can install a gas boiler. Unless you want prosecuting, leave gas installation to an expert. You can probably get yourself into enough trouble in this lifetime without heading gung-ho into this landmine-filled territory of legislation and expert certification.

To save on future energy bills, underfloor heating was used. Underfloor heating systems consist of pipes from the boiler circulating hot water evenly in coils of pipe from room to room under the floor. Underfloor heating is meant to be great because it is efficient but in practice you ultimately need thin floors so heat is not lost in the concrete surrounding the pipes. You'll also need radiators to dry clothing in the centuries-old manner. Forget fancy leaflets and use your head, if something seems like a miracle it usually is. Unless you can find a victim, sorry builder, who has done something innovative and made the innovation work consistently don't get involved. And I mean an innovative builder who has fiddled and fiddled with the technology when it goes wrong and his or her opinion is not sponsored by the vendor. My underfloor heating only works on warm days and if I abandon the settee to lie down as close as I can to the floor I can just about feel something like a gentle warmth.

But don't worry, warmth can be achieved by other means. In terms of old school 'tried and tested' technology there is nothing more yesteryear than a wood burning stove. You'll need a never ending supply of wood but in terms of fire making, few will fail at making a blazing, albeit safe, fire in your home. Heat comes almost guaranteed. Failing that, there's always one, centuries-old sure fire winner – whisky. Whisky will cure stomach bugs, cuts, settle you in times of crisis and even keep you warm. It should really be part of building regulations that each home should have 1 or even 10 bottles of whisky lying around for emergencies.

As the electrics were being installed, the wood fire stove arrived. The wood stove was incredibly heavy and needed a lot of man-handling into place. What I didn't realise, in the paraphernalia that came with the stove there was a missing item. The fire proof, chimney flume to go inside my chimney breast and up to the roof. It was missing. The old timer who sold me the stove had not quoted me for a 'full job'. The much promised flue that avoids suffocating everyone in the room and takes the smoke in a fire proof way up through to the chimney was missing. I rang the old timer who sold me the wood burner to find out where the missing part had got to.

He proudly informed me "That flue was extra".

"Extra?" I said, "Essential more like! How much is the flue? I've paid £1,500 so far and need the final two metre pipe to finish the fire".

"Actually you need me to quote you for fitting too. Otherwise your building insurance will be invalid".

I'd been done by a professional. I was stuck. "How much will the fitting cost? How much for the piece of pipe?"

"£1,000 to fit and £500 for the piping", he confidently replied. I think he sensed a victim on the other end of the phone line.

"You what!? The £1,500 was for 'all in' you said!" I exclaimed in reply.

"No I didn't", he smugly answered.

"I'll think about it", I said and put the phone down.

I needed time to figure out an alternative solution and get out of the victim zone. I was losing money for stuffing a pipe up an already made hole for a chimney. I mentioned this situation to the builder.

The builder's experience was going to pay off again. A two hundred pound flue was purchased from a rival wood stove provider. And a call to the council for an inspector to sign it as safe for the insurer came in at a more reasonable one hundred and fifty pounds. The builder solved the stove problem quickly and to my relief, reasonably cheaply.

The water connection would be a different matter.

Connecting up water pipes to the main supply and then dividing it around the home and the boiler system took a lot of co-ordination. The co-ordination had to work in tandem with the deliveries of the bathroom suite for the main bathroom, ensuite mini bathroom and a downstairs toilet plus kitchen supplies such as the sink and washing machine. Plus I would have to factor in the tiling of the rooms which would be cut around the pipes and other water structures.

There was only one solution and luckily the plumber accepted the challenge - to install the water pipes, bathroom furniture, tile the floor and wall as a complete operation together. This should have been the end of the problem, however, it was not.

The tiles my fiancée had set her heart upon were unbelievably hand made in Italy. And it turned out that our calculations of how many handcrafted tiles we needed were wrong. That led to gaps in the main bathroom whilst a fresh tile order went all the way to Italy and back.

The bathroom handles of some items also fell off. I imagined that I or my fiancée might be sat on a toilet when a faulty toilet seat would give way leaving one of us sitting actually in the toilet bowl. Or that in flushing the toilet, the toilet handle would break leaving the toilet to continually fill and fill. That is, until its mucky contents were happily sailing out of the bathroom door and onto the carpets of neighbouring rooms. Or that pipes might even go missing and spring a sewage splurging leak somewhere. Pipes were a worry for more reasons than one.

During any building it is really important to hide the copper heating pipes. Building sites are renowned for attracting thieves and thanks to an episode of the BBC Apprentice where the challenge was to recycle steel, copper and lead the word was out - copper per kilo was like gold. Copper on its own was valued at a price that made thievery worthwhile and profitable. All copper piping was to be used as soon as it arrived and bolted firmly into place. Any other copper pipes were hidden when not in use or disguised to prevent it disappearing in the night.

Finally, pipes fitted, the simple utility pleasures were in. My fiancée and family stood in the still bare interior of the barn and marvelled at the water coming out through the taps. We gawped at solitary, light bulbs being turned on and off, stood almost mesmerised by flushing toilets and the warmth of freshly gas boiled, hot water. Our home was coming to life. Another building stage was complete. Apart from the bare features of the home it was like a machine starting up for the first time, the barn was beginning to live and breathe. The image of a once derelict barn was fading from memory and now more and more features of a home were emerging and working. Like Frankenstein's Monster, the building was being moved on and coming alive.

Next it was time to give Frankenstein's Monster a shave and a makeover. It was time to finish and polish up the outside of the barn by 'pointing' the walls, as well as clear up the craters of abandoned debris and mountains of piled rubble. It was time to give the monster a makeover and tackle the look of the barn whilst we waited for the internal paraphernalia such as kitchen, internal doors and skirting boards to arrive.

Operation tidy out and tidy up was next.

Chapter 13 – Landscaping A War Zone

"The salvage trade has come a long way since Steptoe and Son. It has moved upmarket and is now teeming with the smart set, sniffing out the hottest bargains. An endless stream of architectural gems has passed through Lassco's doors, including a Robert Adam chimney piece for £170,000 or get a hand-thrown flower pot for as little as £1. Anthony Reeve, Lassco's managing director, is confident that people are putting a bit of soul and character back into their homes with old architectural elements and sculptures. Thornton Kay co-founded Salvo, an organisation that works alongside dealers and the police to stem the flow of stolen goods from buildings and gardens, and believes the new, backward-looking trend is largely driven by well-heeled women, who value the quality of old materials".

Shortened from Stuart Penney, Telegraph newspaper, 2005.

When I remember the old black and white films of World War II I used to watch as a child and the wartime stories my Grandad used to tell me; I imagine the images of broken buildings, smashed masonry, discarded and broken wood and seas of mud. When I looked at the area surrounding the barn, as tidy as we could be for a building site, I still imagined the space resembling something like the aftermath of a war. Wooden planks to cross the deep mud from one place to another and paths around piles of redundant rumble adding a trench like feel of war. Building is messy and we certainly had a big mess to tidy up.

Before we could start the big tidy up it was going to be another visit from the architect. I needed the architect to see what we had done in the barn. I needed him to approve of the work and create the all-important report for the bank, to release the next stage of money.

Cash flow was now very tight. Changes at the bank meant I was now paying bills upfront using six credit cards. The bank was reimbursing me only once it had evidence from the architect that everything was okay. Apparently the bank wanted to check that I had not drunk the money away or placed everything on red in a casino another builder had done. The architect was my 'parent' coming to check what the building 'boys' were up to.

Once again in preparation for the architect's visit it was 'dress up' day. We got dressed up in our finest personal protection equipment of hard hats and high visibility vests. Safety railings and unsafe piles of everything and anything were secured. Even an industrial vacuum came out as we rolled out the builder's version of the red carpet. The clothes ruined by contact with a thousand sharp edges, nails and other things designed to snag or claw at our clothing were gone. No longer would the wind blow through holes in the knees of my jeans and out through the seat of my pants. We were going to look great on this 'dress up' day.

Things were looking good and when the architect arrived he was impressed. I think when I first spoke to the architect the previous year he had had some reservations. Our odds of success were somewhere between the chances of Donald Trump becoming a saint at the Vatican or Tunisia hosting the Winter Olympic Games. The architect questioned my knowledge of all things building and I think he secretly expected us to fail. However, I sensed a change. The architect had moved from concerned parent managing a young, errant child to a proud father talking to an adult son. He had warmed to the barn and was talking to me as an equal. The technical language the building world was using I now understood and the architect was finally warming to us all. Admittedly, he did spend most of the time praising the builder and to be fair his ability to solve supply issues and work around my bank situation was impressive. The barn was going to be a very good first attempt at a home and was very likely to be completed despite my novice status, small budget and complete absence of emergency funds.

The architect duly left satisfied. All was well. He signed off the build stage and forwarded a copy of his report to me. Now I had this report it was time to engage my other building amusement - chasing the bank. I'd launch into my pay day routine of trying to find and then chase up my elusive branch mortgage advisor. I needed to release the next chunk of construction money to pay for the last stage of construction.

A major area where new builds can save money is on labour-intensive work such as repointing the old stone work. If I could take out the centuries-old mortar, the building team would replace it with new mortar. This would make the old walls look consistent with the newly built walls which had replaced the crumbling parts of the barn's walls. The plan was to take a drill, set it to hammer action, and using a chisel drill bit, slowly and laboriously bash out the old mortar to a depth at which the new mortar could be applied. The new mortar would be applied and then twenty-four hours later the labourer, i.e. me, would go round with an old paintbrush and brush it to produce a smooth finish. Completing this labour-intensive work would take days but because I was going to be the one doing the donkey work, a lot of money by the hour could be saved.

Repointing stone work is much easier said than done. Just thinking about this task I can still feel the vibration of the drill in my hands. It took days and days and days, slowly chiselling away the old mortar. I used to go to bed dreaming of chiselling the mortar away. Inevitably my subconscious self would automatically dip back into visions of removing mortar each night after work. Physically it was tough.

Lifting a heavy, ten kilo drill might sound easy enough but applying the drill to the wall with some pressure for hours at a time was not. My forearms would burn with the exertion. Crippling headaches were the norm as the tensed muscles around my shoulders and neck strangled the oxygen going to my head. But this was no time to be soft. I had a job to do and money to save.

Eventually, all the mortar was off. The new mortar was applied between every stone, nook and cranny and then it was ready for a much easier job - paint brushing the mortar smooth. Again this brushing took days and days but this time against the clock.

If the mortar was smoothed too early after being applied it simply came away from the wall on your paint brush. If it was smoothed beyond the ideal twenty-four hour time limit, the set mortar would forever look like it had been flung into place. Ideally, I got to the mortar between twelve and twenty hours of it being laid and this was perfect. The finish looked amazing and like something out of a posh magazine. I could stand there for hours beholding my hard work. I felt impressed by how tidily the new mortar fitted between the old stone that made up my barn's walls. I was amazed and then my own site supervisor arrived...

My fiancée, the other site supervisor, looked at the gable end of the barn on the west side. Traditionally, if you spot a lot of barns, one end is usually rendered over completely with a thick layer of cement all the way across the wall and not just in between the stones. The reason is simple - weather proofing. In this valley, the worst weather always came from the west. Farmers knew this so they would mortar over the entire west end of their barns to prevent dampness and the weather from penetrating the fabric of the building. Now my fiancé had plans for removing the cement render.

"The cement all over the wall doesn't match the other walls", she observed.

"It doesn't need to", I replied, and I explained to her the history and traditions behind mortaring over the entire west end of the barn.

"It looks silly though. I've never seen other buildings in magazines look like this. I think you should take it off", she stated as her eyes rolled over the west end of the barn.

It was a messy looking, patchwork quilt of mortar and there were gaps where the mortar had long since dropped off. I knew what she meant. The cement render looked a mess but could be patched over I reasoned.

My fiancée wanted rid of it all but I didn't want to do any more chiselling or cement paint brushing. I didn't want to have to remove the entire side of mortar. I could feel the aches in my arms agreeing with me. However, as we discussed this, her family joined her on the site and the building team also stopped work to say "hello".

A conversation began between the builders and my fiancé's family and I became invisible. Finally they agreed, "The wall looks silly, get it tidied up, Dave" was the verdict. Another week of grinding hard work was set in motion for me.

After weeks of labouring it was almost a relief for me to get off the scaffolding, put my drill down and go onto another task. The removal of the roof and replacement with new wood beams had left a forest of rotten timbers and wooden debris across the field at the back of the barn. It was time to tidy these timbers up but also to select some of the beams that were in better condition to act as lintels and door features inside the barn.

Most of the abandoned wooden beams were rubbish and were heading directly to the 'firewood' pile of building debris. Over the centuries, the wood beams and rafters had served the barn faithfully but they were now beyond repair. There was no future use for these timbers beyond heating the barn through the wood stove. I collected all of the waste wood together and organised it into a stack. Some of the more intact beams would, however, be handy.

I selected some of the useful beams which I thought were most impressive. Some had interesting details on such as Roman numerals from when the beams were still parts of wood hulled ships. I thought the Roman numerals would create a great talking point for visitors to the barn. I'd be able to explain the build by numbers technique boatyards used to create ships centuries ago. I wire brushed down some of the huge fifteen inch thick, hand carved beams, got rid of all the centuries of dust and sprayed on some preservative to prevent any further woodworm or decay. The beams would be impressive over the internal doors and windows. They had a maze of intricate patterns in the wood grain. The spiralling and wandering shapes in the wood were almost spellbinding and beautiful. The bigger beams must have been from enormous trees growing over centuries. I was going to preserve these huge beams for future generations.

The barn also had a lot of rubble around. It usually costs two hundred pounds per large skip to take away rubble. To save money, the majority of the rubble was cleverly used as foundations for the new drive to the barn. The sheer amount of stone the drive could consume was phenomenal. It was like witchcraft watching large loads of stone simply vanish day after day as they poured tonnes and tonnes of stone into a line of mounds before a digger crushed and rolled the piles flat. Extra stone had to be brought onto the site to continue constructing the driveway through the sea of mud. The bill for extra stone and then crushing it into a drive cost five thousand pounds. The new driveway involved over twenty tonnes of extra stone. This was in addition to the tonnes of masonry we already had from redundant walls removed from the barn. Mud was now a big enemy.

Any building site, especially in the North West needs draining. Our site was again like a war zone. The sea of mud was almost impassable unless you had a lot of horsepower and big tyres. The coming and going of big machinery, hauling bricks and other heavy loads were too much for the saturated ground. Heavy vehicles had left large trenches two or three feet deep in places criss-crossing the land. Wooden boards were laid across the mud where machinery had gouged out huge wheel marks. Walking from one place to another on the wooden boards reminded me of the old images of World War I trenches. We were lucky enough not to be drowning in mud like those poor wartime souls but drop a tool and it was lost. Lost for good. Anything dropped was soon buried in the mud or hidden in the pools of clay coloured water.

It was now time to build our own trenches. In honour of the Dutch, there is a drainage system called the Dutch drain. The Dutch drains would be trenches dug by machines at a depth of six feet deep and then filled with twenty millimetre limestone chippings. At the bottom of the trench would be a wide diameter drainage pipe that connected the Dutch ditch to the nearest farm drain. The Dutch drains would keep surface water from running down the hills, down the field in which my barn sat, and flooding the barn.

A contractor was hired to dig the drains. I didn't fancy digging the ditch by hand in the pouring rain. Two ditches parallel to the back of the barn would defend the building from an attack by water. The diggers soon dug the ditches and even crashed into other buried features underground.

The old cottage that had long since been stripped of stone to build nearby homes including that of Mrs Interfering was found. The cottage had last been occupied in the early 1800s and was adjacent to my surviving barn. Now some long forgotten parts of tea cups, plates and masonry were brought to the surface once more by the diggers. A rusty knife and cup were brought up. They were retrieved by heavy machinery and not in the delicate, hand brushing loving trowel style of a 'BBC Time Team' archaeologist. Fascinating as they were, there would be no eBaying of these barely recognisable items. They were crushed by centuries spent underground and by the many hundred horsepower of a JCB digger. Old water pipes were also dug through. These then needed replacing to avoid creating impromptu fountains on wet days. Things were getting tidier and now drier.

Tidying up also included the roof debris. It was time to collect all the stone flags or slates from the old barn roof. The stone flags were worth money as either patio feature stones or replacement parts on other buildings where stone flags were still used as roofing materials. Some buildings due to preservation orders or being listed buildings (buildings preserved for generations to come by strict planning permission orders) were forced to use stone flags. This was despite their heavy weight, in order to maintain the look and character of a building for future generations. The market was actually quite large for the stone. Indeed my barn would use some of these stone flags power washed off, sealed with water sealant and then cemented into my kitchen floor and hallway. In time this would be a mistake as mentioned before.

The stone flags would also be used for the bottom of window sills in both my house and my brother's later renovation of his house. Using a stone cutter the stone could be cut into squares and make an interesting addition to a rustic looking barn. Again they'd be another talking point for visitors to the barn I mused. They were also a way of cutting costs and avoiding a trip to the shops for tiles.

Unfortunately the softer sandstone of the valley meant we didn't know how easily they would crack up under foot. Even when sprayed with a hard gloss varnish, the stone flags had a tendency to see edges break off. Sometimes you have to pay for hard, well finished tiles or you could opt for York stone which is very hard wearing but expensive. Expensive becomes a problem, especially on an open building site. It was not uncommon in some places for these stone flags to disappear.

Thievery is common on even a completed building site. There is a danger that if the site looks too tidy or if people start to hear about the completion of a building project, thieves might turn up in the night to make things magically disappear. The preferred way to magic items away is to use the anonymous (and usually stolen) white transit van. Apparently, according to Neighbourhood Police, Ford Transits are the vans most criminals prefer due to a sporty 2.5 litre engine on roughly what amounts to a well-built car chassis frame. Cornering with your stolen loot and getting away via the nearest motorway with your powerful engine is made easier thanks to Ford.

The list of things looted from building sites is an eye opener. The work-shy will happily steal a van to collect anything of value and I mean anything. Another nearby building site had paving stones removed safe in the knowledge that the house had yet to be occupied and was minus prying eyes. My builder had a number of tales about unloading his van even in daylight hours and within moments somebody else trying to unload the same van too. It seemed that looting buildings even outside a war zone was common.

Our building site was safer than most because it was at the end of two houses on a shared drive. The intrepid work-shy would have to sneak up past occupied homes after the day's building had concluded and load the van knowing that a simple call to the farm would see a tractor or even Mrs Interfering's car block them in. Farms had a double-edged sword. The fact most farms had a shot gun or many shot guns made thieves wary of a trigger-happy, disgruntled farmer. Unless you were planning on robbing a bank, in which case the opposite is true, as for some a farm represents a relatively isolated, weakly defended arsenal of fire arms.

Over the course of the build I ran up a number of times to the barn fearing a stranger was looting the place, only to find it was a visitor of a nearby house or somebody my dad had sent from the farmyard to 'go and have a look'. I'd even hidden or dropped a cricket bat or golf club behind a nearby wall so when I was faced with friendly faces I didn't look half deranged and crazy sprinting, weapon in hand, to defend the barn.

Ironically Mrs Interfering and her constant interest in my business was probably keeping the property safe. She challenged anyone coming up the shared drive towards the barn with the type of presence reserved only for the military guarding an army base.

The battles to convert the derelict barn finally felt like they were coming to an end. It had been just short of a year. There had been numerous battles with lenders, the weather, errant suppliers, neighbours and the barn itself. At times it felt like the barn was fighting to prevent its return from a wreck to a modern, usable building. We even had casualties needing medical attention and trenches literally to dig. But battles lost and won it felt like the war was coming to an end.

It would turn out everything experienced so far would be the easiest part of the barn conversion. The future held something much more difficult in store. The war wasn't won, it was just getting started. Mrs Interfering would see to that.

Chapter 14 – A Wedding And A Fight

*"There's a lot to think about when it comes to planning a wedding –
photographer, catering, flowers, dress, to name but a few. But what
does the average wedding cost in the UK? The latest figures show that
the average person is going to end up spending £27,161 on their big
day. A survey of 4,000 brides showed that it's venue hire that comes out
as one of the biggest costs. Closely followed by the honeymoon. If you
don't know anyone who has a barn, a marquee or a great hall then the
venue is one cost you probably can't avoid. You can't get married
wherever you want. There are laws that dictate where a marriage in the
UK can happen, so you will need to pay out for an official venue. The
average venue cost comes in at £4,354. However, there are of course
venues that will be significantly cheaper if your heart isn't set on a
stately home".*

Adapted from Colin Rowe, Money Advice Service 2018.

Bigger things were starting to loom on the horizon now. My long-
suffering fiancée now needed to see more of me after my building
enforced absences. And for good reason. Why? Because we had set a
date to get married and that date was now only in three months' time.
Straightaway you can probably guess by a line in the quote above about
mentioning barns as wedding venues, that I had an idea. Cost-cutting
Dave had a devious plan but no, you'd be wrong, we wouldn't be
getting married at home.

The wedding plans were safely in the hands of my fiancée. She studied
every wedding magazine probably not unlike most girls for years. If
there was a wedding service or feature that she didn't know then it
probably didn't exist. If she sat a degree level exam on weddings she
would be down for a 'first classification'. It was time for me, the

husband-to-be, to get involved in the wedding planning domain that my fiancée was leading. It was time to help with the wedding and that meant trips to wedding fairs and the paraphernalia of must have, glitzy and ultimately expensive, one day only services.

The first stop for anyone planning on getting married is to visit a wedding fair. Here you are introduced to an entire industry you have never heard of before; from baker and candle maker, to violinist, party DJ, master of ceremonies, car hire, venue hire, suit hire and anything else you want to spend your money on. Typically the prices are treble what you'd normally expect to pay because they've all got that magic word involved in them - the word 'wedding'.

The sales pitches were slick and well-rehearsed. The wedding fair industry had the same professionals, suppliers and designers heading from one wedding fair to the next, season after season. Each wedding fair provided a host of exhibitors and stalls to visit. Invariably free things such as food tasting and free slices of cake were provided as bait for customers. I always 'filled my boots' on freebies - especially on cake at each wedding fair. Until eventually I realised, and so did each cake maker, I'd been eating the same cakes time after time from the same exhibitors across each wedding fair. We never needed a cake as my fiancée's sister was a highly skilled and qualified baker. On one occasion I was caught munching freebies and one cake maker scolded me like an errant school child and my embarrassed fiancée dragged me away. I could tell that a wedding fair was a serious, stressful, and busy affair. I'd have to get my game face on or risk more withering looks from my fiancée, her chief bridesmaid and anyone else there who I dared not take seriously.

Car wise, I realised I must have been in the wrong industry. Most firms approached by my fiancée months and months previously were all booked. No cars were available for the day we were looking for. That's no mean feat. One car company in Chorley had forty wedding cars so presumably had all forty cars out on wedding duty on the same day as our wedding. Each car was hired out for four hundred pounds and more per day; netting by my estimations, a hefty sixteen thousand pounds in one day! Supplying weddings with cars looked like a fun job. A job driving fast Ferraris or vintage cruising nostalgia around all day everyday, with the added benefit of each vehicle being a money making machine, sounded great!

Wedding venue wise my fiancée already had ideas. Tongue-in-cheek I tried to sell my idea of a cheap wedding at home. After all, if the barn didn't fall down and if I got it tidied up in time we could have a barn wedding. It would be at a fraction of the cost of all the other barns hosting weddings and I knew an outside caterer. The stern looks I received in riposte suggested that this banter to lighten the mood was not going down well. It was time to focus back on the honeymoon, which was my domain, and of course the barn.

I loved planning for the honeymoon. It was touch and go as to which I enjoyed the most - the barn building or planning the trip of a lifetime. A honeymoon was a chance to push the boat out. After all I was getting married, I was only going to get married once and there are still some really great places that I want to see that I wouldn't normally be able to afford to go to. I had seen Las Vegas and Los Angeles on TV so many times that I couldn't not go. Similarly my fiancée wanted to visit San Francisco so a trip to the three different cities was organised for our honeymoon. We would see everything we had seen on TV such as the Grand Canyon, mega casinos, the Baywatch beach in the TV show, Hollywood and Alcatraz plus much more. It was literally going to be a once-in-a-lifetime trip. It was going to be amazing and certainly a break from the busy school year with the building work squeezed in between!

I also had a stag do to plan. An age-old honour which was a great excuse to drink too much in a new place I'd never been to before with twenty of my best friends. It was going to be exciting and different. For some of my friends it would be like digging out your passport to head overseas as we left Lancashire and headed into the Yorkshire countryside. We were headed to the ends of the world for some as we ventured over the border into Yorkshire and the picturesque town of Skipton. We went Land Rover off-roading first with a mass of high powered, turbocharged Range Rovers and Land Rover Defenders.

The Land Rover experience was an eye opener. The experience was far from recklessly tearing around the countryside and bouncing at speed over the testing ground they had set up. This event was going to be a skilful and challenging affair of control, power and bravery. Far from the wheel spinning approach Jeremy Clarkson would favour to get in and out of mud and more mud, the instructors showed us more than just power. They showed you how to submerge the cars past their bonnets in streams and how to drive down hills so steep only your seatbelt stopped you falling through the front windscreen and down the bonnet into the mud. The vehicles could seemingly defy gravity on some hills and go where I probably wouldn't even go with a tractor. I started to wonder why we had tractors at all until I asked about the cost of one of the three tonne Range Rovers. A mobile armchair set high and dry on a turbo-charged, three tonne monster would set you back two tractors each or eighty thousand pounds.

The most important feature was the speed. And as it was my stag do the staff allowed me to use the 'chav button'. The chav button is a button that revs the engine, perfects the suspension, and makes the car accelerate for you like a NASA space launch. It was alleged the chav button – officially called 'Launch Control' was jokingly designed for racing. Namely, for when some scally (or chav as they call them in my neck of the woods) pulls up next to you at traffic lights and wants a race. Usually the chav will race you leaving you humiliated at the hands of his body kitted, low slung, wide wheeled wreck of a car. When he thinks he is going to race you off the mark, you press the chav button and watch the cannabis joint drop from his gawping mouth as you vanish into the distance. You will have left him for dust while his gaggle of halfwits drop their cans of supermarket own brew all over his car in surprise. I tried the chav button and it flung the three tonne Range Rover at lightning speed down the special road at Land Rover. The acceleration was ballistic!

I was sold on the vehicle despite never in my lifetime ever having the money to buy even a cheap, high mileage, decade-old version. But next came the main event - food and beer.

Lots of beer and then the bleary-eyed breakfast with the stag do survivors the morning after. So many survivors whose only recollection of the night before would be out of focus photographs on mobile phones or receipts from ill-advised trips to cash machines throughout the night. Anyway I'm heading off task, so back to the story of building my own home.

The stag do was ticked as completed and I was back at the barn. At last, when I thought summer couldn't get any wetter and weather records were being broken, we started to see the sun. Sunny days were starting to cast a warm glow over the barn. I could almost taste the barbecues. I could almost feel the sunny days relaxing in the garden. Hopefully the grass would have grown back by then and out of the building debris I could dream that a nice sunny garden would eventually appear. A garden in which I could do something completely unrelated to building anything. My sunny garden vision was inspiring to me.

When you build your own home you need to have a vision that motivates you. A vision of where you are going and what you need to do that helps keep you focused and motivated. You'll need this vision when at times things would challenge you. My vision of success was that in future summers we'd have lots of friends and family over drinking, listening to music and having a barbecue in our garden. The barn would be complete and would have hanging baskets of flowers hung from each corner of the building. Wild flowers and clematis creepers with bright purple flowers would cover walls and everything would look warm and peaceful. The sky would be clear and blue with great vistas across the valley up to Pendle Hill in the distance and across the valley to the historic castle which sits calmly above Clitheroe. The garden would have borders of plants and eventually we'd have a patio edged with yet more flowers and above it, covered by a wood railed gazebo, creeping plants flowering in the sun. There would be lots of people and lots of flowers basically. And it would be sunny.

However, Mrs Interfering had other plans. She was more intent than ever to prevent my barn and flower plans from moving from my imagination and becoming reality. She had now announced that empty legal threats to my visitors and her car-based blockade would extend. Her new decree was that delivery trucks were no longer to come up the shared drive because they were catching her precious branches. The branches were overhanging the shared drive from her garden and defending her sprawling branches she would turn visitors around in the lane and stand in the way to prevent access. I secretly hoped that given her diminutive stature that a big wagon might not see her and simply drive over the top of her on the way in and again on the way out.

I spoke to Mrs Interfering politely but unfortunately the dictator had ruled. Instead, I checked with the council and with my solicitor. The vans were indeed catching branches and there was an issue. However, we also had the right to use the drive until the building was complete and a new, alternative drive had been installed. We were also within our rights to cut back the branches to the boundary fence. And then under law, required to return the offcuts in a tidy pile to her.

The laws were interesting. The intricacies of the law meant that everything was okay as long as we didn't take any fruit from the overhanging branches (There was no fruit anyway) and if we returned all the branch clippings to their rightful owner. I'm guessing this originates from the wood fire days when this wood would have to be needed to keep the owner warm.

A polite letter was written to Mrs Interfering asking her to cut the branches in the next fortnight or, failing that, we could do it for her if she wanted. She declined to reply so two weeks later we returned with a tractor, a trailer and a saw. Mrs Interfering was ready with a camera to record what she saw as a deviation from her decree. Under her careful watch, we cut back the branches. Now there would be no problem with the deliveries but unfortunately I was wrong again.

The kitchen mentioned in an earlier chapter now finally began to arrive. The kitchen pieces arrived over a number of weeks. The first would arrive shortly after the branch cutting.

The first kitchen delivery arrived. Mrs Interfering's daily roadblock of her car parked across my gateway had expired at 5:30pm. Her car was now safely parked away in its garage just as my delivery truck arrived. This time the delivery was the expensive double oven designed to be the focal point of the kitchen.

Luckily, the shared access was now wide open and delivering the oven looked like an easy task. Simply drive up, park the van, drop off the ovens and then we'd wheel them into the barn. The van would drive off, mission accomplished. However, there was a Mrs Interfering in the plan.

Mrs Interfering was sprightly for an elderly person and literally ran to her garage to get her car out. After many years of reversing her car out, she was there in place, within seconds. Now the heavy ovens risked a trip all the way around to the other drive which at this point was still being compressed into a driveable surface by heavy machinery. Mrs Interfering was asked if she would move her car for us. I had by now checked the law with my legal advisor and I now knew that you couldn't legally park across a right of way for longer than forty-five minutes.

Instead, she refused to move her car and sat at the window of her kitchen watching what would happen next. The heavy but delicate double oven would have to be lifted over the top of her small car and brought to my home. The difficult job was managed eventually but Mrs Interfering was angry. Angered that she had been defeated and so her son was called and he would be the short-tempered, angry one of her two sons. Things were escalating as we kept overcoming everything Mrs Interfering was throwing at us.

Mrs Interfering's oldest son was a tall man short-tempered and somebody I'd soon see quite regularly. He stormed into the farmyard and demanded to see me. After some shouting at my brother and my father he realised I wasn't around. I was at school marking books oblivious to the tempers flying back at home.

It wouldn't be long before I was face to face with the angry son of Mrs Interfering, I'd seen the other son on CCTV but now I would see the other son in person. It was the Easter holidays and I was taking my mum away as tradition dictated on Good Friday to a place of her choosing for a day out. A nice, relaxing day out. As I was helping my mum into my car Mrs Interfering's son saw me in the street.

He was furious. He yelled at volume that his Mum had parked where she wanted on that drive for many, many years and she would not be changing that anytime soon. He also told me that I was going to do things his way and that would be the end of it. I should not access the drive and no one else should come up that drive, he continued to command.

He had, however, picked the wrong man to scream and rave at. After managing a number of Toys R Us stores I had to re-trained as a teacher and I had worked in some tough schools before the nice leafy school I now worked at. I was used to people getting in my face, threatening and swearing at volume. I was head of a school department and had been sent by my colleagues more than my fair share of screaming teenagers. In some cases these angry pupils were well over six feet tall and violent. Mrs Interfering's son would be no different in my eyes.

I stood up to him and told him my point of view. I had legal advice and now I even had my own free legal advisor from the bank's legal insurance. I suggested that before this went any further, Mrs Interfering's son should speak to his mother to sort things out because things were going to get out of hand. I told him things would probably head to court. He seemed stunned.

His shouting game had not had the effect it was meant to. I'd seen bullying tricks played out many times in the playground and 'weight throwing' by teenagers. When Mrs Interfering's son walked towards me and shouted, I took a few steps closer, cut the distance and he stopped. It was the alpha male trick, the dominant stand their ground. The weaker step back and encourage the dominant male to get even louder and more aggressive in their demonstration of authority. He was not going to intimidate me and he knew it. Short of trying to punch me or simply shouting louder he was all out of his negotiating tactics. It had almost killed me putting my home together and some mouthy individual was not going to stop me finishing it now.

With the adrenaline still pumping I went away to enjoy Good Friday in the Lake District. I could never realise how fateful my last words of "things will get out of hand" to Mrs Interfering's son would be. Trouble was brewing and I sensed I would be gaining more than my existing penfriends at the bank.

Letters were starting to go regularly to the council from the architect's practice Mrs Interfering had specially hired to 'investigate and monitor' me. While this seemed extreme, things in what I would call 'neighbourhood circus' were about to implode. We would all be heading to the Big Top and performing at the main stage with an audience looking on.

In this audience there would be people wearing uniforms, have handcuffs and work at a police station. No longer would the police visit from the community beat or neighbourhood policing team. Eventually the falling out would lead to an arrest and a whole new experience. The usual solicitors' letters I expected and was now becoming familiar with were about to also require a new type of solicitor. I was about to move from civil law and get involved in criminal law and prison time...

I was about to get arrested.

Chapter 15 – A Lesson In Interior Design

"Our opportunity, as designers, is to learn how to handle the complexity, rather than shy away from it, and to realize that the big art of design is to make complicated things simple. The life of a designer is one of fight: fight against the ugliness".

Massimo Vignelli, Italian Designer & Architect, 1950.

When you watch designers on TV I just find them to be airy, fairy and not easy to understand. They often wore bright, oddly assembled clothes in order to look edgy. They talked about the 'feel' of a room and what the room 'embodied'. I always imagined when talking about the 'feel' of a room of closing my eyes, laying my hand on the wall and then blindly walking into anything and everything. Shows with Laurence Llewelyn-Bowen always seemed to be trying to improve some home which in his opinion was drab, but to me the homes looked fine. In my opinion they often looked better before he applied the garish colours he favoured painting in.

At the start of my building project I had sorry-looking timbers, damp walls and centuries of dust. Any thoughts of choosing curtain colours or talking about what a room embodied were non-existent. I had no thoughts about rooms beyond a number preceded by a pound sterling sign, interior design was one area that was not on my mind.

Luckily for me then, my fiancée was really keen on this area. The interior details of the barn mattered to her. This works well as a partnership as I had little idea and little interest beyond finding a place to live in that would be comfortable, not fall down and not embarrass me when friends came to visit. When looking at timbers that had seen more woodworm than wood or created more resulting 'saw dust' from their chewing than a sandpit had seen sand, the idea of drapes and complementary colours was far from my thoughts.

Bigger things were still precluding any thought of interior design. It was just two months before the wedding and the bridge connecting the two halves of the upstairs floor still needed its final makeover. The bridge had scared many people because it was quite narrow at a metre and a half wide and three metres long with a sheer drop down each side into the living room below. For some this bridge was exciting, for others it was suicidal to cross unless you were one of the builders accustomed to crossing the open bridge. The bridge went past the big glass windows which replaced the open gap where tractors and trailers came and went. To keep as much light coming in to the barn as possible the balustrades for the bridge would be sheets of toughened glass. Sheets of glass were used to both look nice but also allow as much light as possible to cascade into the barn's main living area. It was time to put these panels into position.

When the glass panels finally arrived it was not all plain sailing. Some of the pieces were missing. The glass panel hand rails also required far more construction than anticipated. We expected that the glass metre square sheets would have already been fitted to their fixtures on delivery and then would have simply fastened the fixtures on either side of the bridge. This was not going to be the case.

As a wise boss once reminded me - frequently - to assume is to make an ass of you and me. He explained that to make an ASS of U and ME was the sole cause of all disasters. Think things through and foresee every 'pratfall' as he called the 'unexpected'. The glass panels would be a great example of making an ASS of U and ME. The glass panels were not ready. Instead it would be a much more difficult, and potentially disastrously costly, as it was a matter of gently forcing the glass into position. With rubber mallets, the glass would be coaxed into thin, rubber lined, steel troughs. The troughs had to be pre-positioned and fastened to either side of the bridge.

Gently forcing the glass panes into the troughs with the builder was a painstaking and frightening task. The cost of the glass was high and with one wrong move it could smash and laminate into a million pieces. Under the stress, gripping the glass with your bare hands was a slippery, sweat-inducing operation that lasted for hours. The glass was toughened but like all toughened glass it was only very strong if you hit it in the middle of a panel and not the Achilles' heel of its edges. It would be exactly in those edges where we would be coaxing the glass to slide into its final resting place using a rubber mallet. If the job wasn't enough to make us sweat, the huge windows nearby would be. Being next to the large windows, it was like sitting in a greenhouse and the sweat was running off our foreheads. One wrong move or mistake and it would be another four week wait and an expensive bill for a replacement sheet of glass. And now we were baking in the sun too.

It took forever to manage the glass into place. The six sheets which made up the glass replacement for the traditional railings you'd expect on a landing or balcony took all day to install. At the end, after a long day, there was an issue. There was a small gap and this needed another piece of glass at ninety degrees to the last piece to bridge this gap. The glass on the bridge also needed fixing into the walls at either end of the bridge. The problem was that now the last remaining glass fasteners were missing. We couldn't make the glass railings safe.

I called many times to the office in Nottingham who supplied us with the glass and fittings. All I needed were the two ninety degree fasteners plus the wall to glass fasteners. Each time the receptionist or the boss said he or she would call back to let me know when the parts would be on their way. Apparently the parts I needed were only available in Germany and the fact that they made the glass panels meant that the German firm was the only one in the world that could supply the correct fixtures. Fixtures that would not damage the glass but hold it securely. Each time I rang to chase the parts I was left waiting days and days. I rang again and again to continue the circle of 'remind the supplier, supplier re-orders, German company apparently has no record of the order, so remind the supplier of the order, the supplier re-orders...' and well, you get the idea.

Other ideas floated across my mind but none were any good. Machining custom, bespoke fasteners would be time consuming and hugely expensive. Even more expensive when a slight measurement could render the fasteners useless if they failed to fasten in the correct gaps and pre-drilled holes in the glass. I started to search the internet to find a local supply for the glass clasping devices.

At last I found a glass merchant whose website said they had the parts. Better still, they operated very nearby – that was an excellent break in my mind! So after work I decided to nip to the next village across from mine to buy and collect the pieces.

The glass panel merchant was just locking up his small unit on an industrial estate. It had a lot of different company names on the side of his unit but one of them said something about glass so I decided to enter. The office staff were just leaving, presumably to go home for tea whilst the boss give a quick end of the day tidy of his desk.

I explained what I needed. I showed him pictures of the glass panels and where in the glass panels the fixtures would be needed. He said he was surprised that they weren't already supplied with the glass panels. Even more surprised as the fittings would have been purposely cut to fit the gaps we were looking at. I explained that the Nottingham company hadn't sent the parts and instead they had repeatedly sent an order back to Germany to get the pieces made and redelivered.

"Oh?" The man went suspiciously quiet all at once. The warm, helpful, welcome chat stopped.

"Yes", I continued, "the company was just an office in Nottingham like this one, where the parts aren't made but orders are sent to manufacturers to make parts on their behalf".
"I see...", he listened, intently.
"Yes, it's for a barn conversion at..."I stopped.

I looked around the room. Maps on the wall and computers suggested that it was a small business and I could see no evidence of any glass cutting equipment. There were a few panes of glass lying against desks here and there in the small office unit. Small plastic bagged bundles of nuts, bolts and other fixtures lay around. There was a change in the man's demeanour. He backed away to sit on his desk, only his backside couldn't hide the obvious. I saw brightly and clearly a familiar company logo and next to it – a name.

As the boss backed into his desk a magazine fell off the desk. The magazine that dropped down on to the floor was a catalogue of glass parts, pieces and all manner of bespoke glass products used in the building industry. Clearly on top was the name of the Nottingham company I had been dealing with all along.

"IT'S YOU!! I've been chasing you for weeks!!", I shouted with a startle.

I spotted a number of blank letter headed pieces of paper bearing the same company name but this time with a new address, the actual address of the unit I was stood in. He was the man I needed. Far removed from the Nottingham office where I believed he was based and now after countless weeks of being fobbed off repeatedly we were face to face in an empty office on a quiet industrial unit.

Without much more to do, he went to his shelving in a small cupboard and pulled out the parts I needed. He was about to offer his excuses but we both knew nothing was going to cut the ice.

It turns out that online these simple, heavy-duty stainless steel items are expensive but they were quoted as part of the glass cost. In my opinion he tried to sell the same items twice but I could be wrong. Fortunately my luck was in and his luck was out. Now I was going to return home with the pieces I needed. Ironically I was still missing pieces for the ninety degree join on one side but my brother found these and bought the missing steel fittings for my birthday.

The walkway was now made safe by the glass safety panels or as well as they could be with the missing parts. The glass panel flanked walkway was perfect. The glass sides let the vast windows, which replaced the former tractor and trailer entrances, cascade huge amounts of natural light into the upper areas of the barn and across the lower areas such as the living room. We weren't allowed extra windows due to the planning department's insistence. They didn't want the external character of the barn to be lost or the privacy of the all-important Mrs Interfering to be affected. Any new windows were definitely not required now. The light coming through the big windows, unhindered by the glass sided walkway filled the barn well and looked amazing. It was now time for interior design.

Other focal points were now almost complete. The surround around the wood burning stove had now been finished. The stove had a stone surround made up of stone flags behind the fire with the sides now a natural stone hearth crowned by a large oak beamed mantelpiece. The oak mantelpiece was part of one of the huge oak beams that held up the barn's roof for centuries. Inches thick, cleaned up and treated, it now sat across the stone columns that framed the top of the fireplace. Painting was next.

Decoration wise I don't think you can go far wrong with matt white trade paint. White goes with any colour imaginable. If you scrape it, you can very easily paint over with another matt finish white paint and never see the mark again. It's genius and being water-based, it's a very easy paint to use. The paint I was going to be using for the wood skirting boards and doors would be a different matter.

Doors and skirting boards were all being fitted to the house. It was ironic really. I'd been used to climbing into my home through windows when there was no glass and going from room to room without opening and closing doors. Obviously there's a need for doors and not making everything open-plan. It turns out in order to get a building inspector to pass your house you need to have a number of doors in certain places. For example, to stop the spread of a kitchen fire there must be a door from the kitchen to other parts of the house. A lot of door rules make sense because you don't want kitchen smells creeping into the rest of the house and making the place smell like a chippy or a tandoori. Similarly, you want doors on bathrooms so that guests don't feel that anyone is going to pop up and catch them with their pants down literally. And you need doors to stop the moisture escaping from those hot baths and creating the sort of mould that damages lungs over time and eats its way through wooden floor joists. Rotten, damp floorboards are no good to anyone and can be seriously dangerous.

In fact, I had heard of a 'Peeping Tom' crushed to death by mould and dampness. It was on a Sky TV show called "1000 Ways to Die". The 'Peeping Tom' had drilled so many holes into the floor of the apartment above him and around the bathroom in particular, that he'd been killed. In his attempt to ogle the beautiful young girl upstairs he had drilled holes for eye pieces in the ceiling of his apartment and floor here and there. The moisture had caused bacteria to build in the floor joists and floorboards. This in turn had created a mouldy substance capable of eating its way through wood - given enough time. Unfortunately for the Peeping Tom, he was stood underneath a rotted bathroom floor, peeping at his beautiful neighbour whilst she jumped into the bath. The combined weight of both the girl and full bath of water was enough to break through the weakened floor and crush the hapless pervert between his kitchen table and the bottom of her bath. The lesson here -

add doors to your home and stop mould. You can also add vents to your walls especially in bathrooms. Legally for fireplaces you'll need good sources of ventilation too. Especially if you have a wood burning stove otherwise a poorly burning fire will create a silent killer - carbon monoxide. And if you don't have good ventilation or a carbon monoxide detector you too could be appearing on Sky TV's '1000 Ways To Die'.

Anyway, back on track. The doors needed painting. White walls with mahogany doors and skirting boards would be the theme of the house. In our case, the expensive look would be faked using the colour of mahogany painted wood to save money. The best way to make this mahogany effect paint is to use one part oak coloured wood stain and two parts pine wood stain. The effect gives a lovely deep, rich-looking mahogany effect on your hardwood doors and skirting boards. The builder already started the painting with his team but then to save money I relieved them of the painting so that the team could use their expertise to continue cutting more skirting boards to size and fitting doors.

Mixing paint is easier said than done. Invariably each mixture of paint looks different from the last batch. I fully recommend a tip here which is to think big and mix far more than you need. Unpainted wood always absorbs a lot more paint than you think it would. And no matter how accurately you measure together the portions and combinations of paint, witchcraft always seems to make it change to a different colour when you paint it on anything. One batch of mixed paint never seems to blend seamlessly with the previous batch.

I also recommend that you paint the white walls before you put the skirting boards on and also paint skirting boards before you nail them to the wall. That way, no matter how badly you paint, you are unlikely to mess up the skirting boards or walls with drips here and there of the other's paint. You'll also avoid having to remix and reproduce the impossible to copy, homemade mahogany wood stain when you come to hide wall painting drips.

Another thing to think about regarding interior design is storage. Few builders start thinking along the lines - wouldn't it be amazing to put a cupboard here or a shelf there. In reality builders have bigger things to think about such as whether there will even be a wall here or there that you can fasten a shelf to.

In the storage department, it was always a dream of my fiancée to have a walk-in wardrobe. A wardrobe so large, you can walk inside it and hang your clothes in a neat and ordered style just like in the film 'Sex and the City'. A walk-in wardrobe the size of a small room where everything is perfect and everything is easy to access. My fiancée got her dream and ironically it was probably one of the few places in the house where we did actually have storage incorporated in the original plans for the building.

The walk-in wardrobe was a place we would have storage details such as shelving, railings and places to put things down and find them again. Everywhere else, the barn was a sea of boxes and looked like something out of a warehouse. The mess would get worse again when we finally moved in, got rid of all the tools and empty boxes of past building materials to add our personal effects.

The wardrobe was measured by another design company and installed in pieces. Again the delivery company had to avoid Mrs Interfering and took an over the top precaution to walk the pieces, on shoulders, to the barn from the nearest layby in a street away from the barn. The supplier said fitting the pieces of the walk-in wardrobe was actually quicker than bringing it from the van. In reality, he did not want the van to get stuck in our other drive as it was still being constructed. He had also heard tales of the pint size Mrs Interfering patrolling our shared access way from the carpet man laying our carpets.

By now the barn was emerging modern and tidy and just simply needed the kitchen to come in and be fitted ready for the architect's last and final report to release money from the bank. The kitchen was chosen to look like it was made from mahogany and match the rest of the house but with a deep black marble work top. The kitchen would look amazing and be part of the biggest room in the house as we reasoned that after a long day at work we would spend most of our time cooking in the kitchen, and if we were lucky we'd later go through to the living room to relax away the remaining evening before heading to bed.

The kitchen was a beautiful set up but unfortunately I was starting to lose my sense of love for it. The kitchen started to arrive not in days but over a period of weeks. Bit by bit it was slowly delivered but delivered in a way to ensure that there was not enough of it to start work on. I felt that the kitchen delivery schedule was cleverly arranged by its designers to ensure that not one component delivered would match up with any other component. And that somehow neighbouring boxes of useful things would be delivered separately at different times to prevent assembly. I imagined that in the kitchen warehouse there was a great collection of twenty boxes on the floor and staff were sliding and puzzling the boxes around to carefully prevent any one shipment giving us the chance to start assembly. A sort of box shuffling puzzle that an amateur human resources department might frame as a challenge or as part of a team building exercise.

The lack of kitchen was a problem because part of the deal with the bank was that the house would have to be complete before releasing the next payment. The bank's definition of 'completed' included fully working bathrooms and habitable by which the bank meant a fully working kitchen. Not that I needed a kitchen – I told the bank that I'd use my army cadet camping stove if required in order to live in the barn. Despite my useless boast, the bank wasn't interested in any make-shift fire hazard I could offer. Access to a working bathroom was also part of the bank's 'liveable home' equation but luckily for me the plumber had done a great job. I could easily prove to the architect that I could go to the toilet and have a bath - though not at the same time.

I was in serious debt waiting for the kitchen to be installed. The builder had now pretty much finished the house and was well within his rights to demand final payment for a job well done. Except I couldn't pay the bills. My six credit cards were maxed out. I'd gone from a non-credit card using individual to someone who was playing Russian roulette with a number of cards in order to juggle my cash flow crisis. The roulette stakes were high, I was like a desperate player in a poker game trying to maintain my bluff. My bluff was that I was still in the game and had money. I'd need actual real money now and lots of it to get out of my bluff.

The bluff I had money was going to get suddenly more difficult. During the wait for the kitchen to arrive the architect was due to go away for an extended long holiday. I desperately needed the kitchen to all arrive in its many boxes or in a trailer in one huge delivery as soon as possible. By now I was down to the last week of the architect being available and I was at the end of my finances.

Recklessly I booked the architect to visit just before he went on holiday. I reasoned that I could persuade him that the kitchen was not an issue and that the remaining kitchen parts were going to arrive soon. It was then a straightforward job of constructing the units and sliding the equipment such as ovens and freezers into place. The architect could then write up and sign his report for the bank before he went on holiday. To action this plan, I'd go out and get the kitchen myself.

On the day before the architect was due to arrive the kitchen should have been finished. I'd been hit by kitchen delay after kitchen delay but now it was my school half-term. I now had a fighting chance of having a kitchen in place for the architect to sign his report off against. Being off work, I had a week in which I could use all sorts of tactics and cause devilment to ensure the kitchen was delivered before the architect visited.

Foolishly I'd already paid for most of the kitchen so my bargaining position was quite weak. However I was also a desperate fool and needed the money from the bank as soon as possible and the absence of our kitchen was in the way.

The kitchen designers couldn't care less. The designers were more interested instead in designing and selling new kitchens to new customers rather than dealing with an ongoing nuisance like myself. Numerous complaints to the kitchen design company had made very little progress. However I was about to take my school holiday and time off work to make sure I stayed at the forefront of their thoughts. The kitchen designers were about to be motivated to help me.

I visited the kitchen designers' office with my sandwiches first thing on the first Monday of my holiday. I was both mentally and food wise prepared. I wouldn't be leaving until tea time and I'd come prepared with a box of sandwiches because I was now a veteran builder and negotiator. I knew the score. I was going to be belligerent and a nuisance to anyone who wanted to sell anyone a kitchen.

The office was fairly quiet first thing on the Monday morning, so I approached a kitchen designer. I would have gone for my designer but unfortunately she'd left for maternity leave. Unless I wanted to wait for ten months she wasn't coming back anytime soon. The kitchen designer I approached was pleasant but ultimately gave me the standard company fob off, i.e. the parts will turn up *eventually*. I had already been waiting three months and wasn't willing to wait until the end of time or until somebody, somewhere, happened to take pity on my case.

It wasn't long before I got my opportunity to motivate the designers to help with my kitchen cause. A young couple came through the doors to the showroom and I waited for them to get interested in a kitchen.

The couple seemed to settle on a nice kitchen in a very rustic style, a large oak-looking kitchen with flowers and a white top. Once hooked, one of the showroom designers could sense the couple's interest and went over to the couple to begin her sales patter. Keywords took my interest:

"How long will it take to deliver for example?" enquired the boyfriend. Before the designer could reply, I chirped in, "I replied four months and still counting".

The couple looked surprised.
"No it takes two to four weeks at the very most", replied the designer.
"No it doesn't", I said to the designer, "Here's my order form carbon copy. It says this was four months ago". And I thrust my ragged, crumpled order under her nose for all to see.
"Technically they have sent the kitchen in bits over the last eight weeks but no one knows when the last piece will arrive", I added.

The kitchen designer was not impressed by my comment and tried to backtrack on my statement.

"How much discount can you give us if we pay upfront", the girlfriend asked the designer.
"Never pay up front, this is how they trapped me, I'm still waiting for my kitchen pieces. I should have paid at the end, on delivery", I butted in.

By now the couple were regarding me as an oddball and they looked at me with a look reserved for those not sure if someone is dangerous or not. I was desperate, I had no shame. I needed my kitchen I thought to myself. Plus no one here knows who I am, I need my kitchen or I'll be filing for bankruptcy.

They wandered around the showroom with the kitchen designer and I tagged along like an awkward third guest in partnership. Eventually when I started making the couple feel uncomfortable, my work was done. They left, the saleswoman had lost a sale.

I then wandered over to join another couple who had just come through the door.

Luckily for them, the boss had finally heard I was causing problems and tried to beckon me quietly into his office. He gave me an ultimatum, he'd promise to deliver the parts for the kitchen this week if I left or he'd call the police. Plenty of police had already visited my home. Every time I walked up the drive to the barn they were called by Mrs Interfering for one contrived reason or another. Another police encounter no longer put the fear of God into me like it would have done twelve short months ago. To call the boss's bluff I told him I'd stay for the police and I'll tell the officer what the company had done. I said quietly I hoped to get my story in the press as well regarding their customer service and being potentially arrested over this. This would be a consumer protest.

The boss thought for a moment, he was clearly dealing with a situation that needed solving. I had succeeded in putting my consumer protest to the forefront of his priorities. He picked up his phone of his desk and made a few phone calls.

"Okay, I'll go to the warehouse tomorrow. We will make a special delivery by tomorrow night", he promised, "Will that solve this?"

"Thank-you", I agreed and to call his bluff and reaffirm by dedication to the cause, "If not, I'll come back with my sandwiches tomorrow. It's warm in here and I've nothing to do until I get on with building my kitchen".

The boss nervously thanked me and I walked back to the car park. I felt slightly nervous from the adrenaline of being a rebel. I also felt slightly 'sordid' in how I made the young couple feel but also massively relieved. If the kitchen was delivered tomorrow it could be built by Wednesday and inspected by the architect on Thursday. He could write his quick report, and email it to the bank before he went on holiday the following Monday. I could then be writing cheques to pay the bills by a week on Friday.

The kitchen arrived as promised at the end of the following day. The worktop however came from a different manufacturer and it turned out they were based in Birmingham. The worktop manufacturer overestimated their schedule and were apparently unable to visit until the following week. This meant the architect deadline would still be missed.

Thinking on my feet I was beginning to learn negotiation skills when dealing with suppliers. I told them I had already paid for the architect to visit on Thursday. I told them that I wouldn't be able to get the certificates needed for the bank if they didn't complete their job this week.

There was a good chance they would not get paid, they had breached their contract and additionally the architect visit fee money would be lost as the architect would have to revisit again to sign the barn off. Here came my belligerence, I lied about the cost of the architect and told them that they owed me five hundred pounds for his fee as they hadn't done their job as promised. I was going to hammer home that the bill was not mine but theirs due to the error.

I launched into a pressure pitch of my own and I said, "Have you got a pen? I'll need you to transfer the money for the architect's fee to me and I'll give you my bank details".

"Err no", the startled delivery driver replied.

"Get a pen now and here's the number, it will be for five hundred pounds", and I started reading out my account number.

"We don't owe this. We're booked up", they protested.

I let their comments fall on my deaf ears and continued ramping up the pressure, "There might be a fee for the builder too, I'll have to check as he's booked staff ready for your delivery", I continued.

"Actually, it's okay, we'll change a delivery slot. We have one free and we'll be near to you. But it will be around 8pm before we can deliver the kitchen top", he said.

The kitchen work top delivery team was now thinking that I was a builder and that I'd definitely want to go home before that time. He'd calculated wrong and to call his bluff of the late night delivery, I simply replied, "Yes no problem, see you at 8pm".

The delivery boys duly turned up at 8pm. It was going to be a late night and it took three hours to fit the worktop. Some parts had been measured wrongly by the kitchen designer on her first visit to the barn. It was going to take skill and patience to make the worktop fit around the kitchen appliances, windows and doorways.

To give the delivery boys their due, they were tired and worked hard all the way through fitting the heavy, thick marble worktop. The finish looked incredible and the kitchen despite the huge wait and time involved in chasing the parts looked amazing. I now had a habitable house as defined by the bank. I was now ready to greet the architect and accept my final payment from the self-build mortgage to pay the builder plus clear my numerous credit card balances too.

Negotiation skills were getting better and I was starting to be able to project manage like the best of them. I was now on the edge of victory, I could almost taste success! It was time for the architect and the building inspector to review my work.

Chapter 16 – What Have We Done?

"As the job moves forward the Building inspector will usually carry out additional checks. They may need to see the floor and ceiling joists to ensure they are in accordance with the approved drawing. They will want to check the size, grade and centres of the joists, together with any herringbone strutting and restraint strapping. All of the roof timber/trusses may be checked for correct size and grade of timbers at the correct spacing. They will be interested in both thermal and sound insulation to make sure it is of the correct type and thickness. The structural integrity of the building is very important, but equally the fire safety and glazing regulations need to be precisely adhered to. The staircase must conform to several important rules. If there are problems they can be expensive to put right.

Finally a Statutory Inspection 7 - when the building is occupied prior to completion, the local authority needs to be notified to check work is up to government legislated standards. This is usually merged with Statutory Inspection 8. It is important that the inspector has a final walk round to check, ventilation to rooms and roof voids, roof coverings, fire precautions and fire safety, safety glazing, and staircase details and geometry to name a few points".

Adapted from Peter Eade, Homebuilding & Renovation 2017.

I remember when I was a child. I always worked hard and tried my best in everything I did, but I couldn't help but want to know how well was I doing against others my age. In my teaching profession they would euphemistically call this 'peer referencing'. Peer referencing is checking where you are against others so I could either gloat or pull my socks up and work harder. Usually I had to work harder and I remember at primary school I needed to work hard. I was a summer, July born child and I needed a lot more support than most as I was almost a year younger than some of my classmates. However, like most things, with hard work I usually caught up.

My biggest disappointment at school was failing to follow in my Dad's footsteps to the local grammar school. I'd failed my '11 Plus' exam and wasn't considered 'good' enough for the grammar school. Fast forward five years, however, and I was top of my classes at high school and successfully applied to the prestigious sixth form of the same grammar school that turned me down. I'd soon rise to the top of the class in two of my subjects and do respectably well in the other two. The point I'm making is that I needed to compare with others and I craved feedback on my progress. Today was going to be one of those days - it was the day the building inspector was going to visit. The day I was going to find out how well we did.

To end your self-build project you need a final say from the council before you can occupy the building. This comes in the form of your all-important, God-like, building inspector. You cannot legally occupy your house without the say so of the building inspector and today he was going to visit.

Unlike most inspections in life, it's worth speaking to your building inspector as you progress with your build in order to ask their advice and so that you meet their ideals. A bit like a teacher's pet, finding out more and garnering their support for your work. The building inspector's aim is not to prevent you from living in your home but instead to help you build a home that is safe and not likely to fall down around your ears. Then they judge you.

A well-constructed home should be your obvious aim, especially in the inclement Lancashire weather where it usually rains hard in summer, and even harder in winter. Incidentally, anyone who visits Lancashire will hear about its cotton industry rich past. The main reason for locating so many cotton mills here in the past was that it was the dampest part of the entire nation so cotton threads wouldn't dry out and snap. Little has changed in the centuries since. It's still very wet here.

The building inspector arrived on cue. It's wise to consult a building inspector assigned to your build any time you have a question because they are experienced engineers. Unlike the rest of the bureaucracy of the council planning department their remit is to help and advise, not just to terrify or cause further form filling. I was pretty sure the building inspector would pass the home but I wanted to know how well we had done. Would there be any remedial work, would there be any expensive additions or changes required or were we finished and ready for the bank to send more money and wipe out my mountains of debt?

Before I give you the building inspector's answer here's a riddle for you. When is a bedroom not a bedroom? I know what you're thinking. You're thinking along the lines of if something is missing. An easy example would be a bedroom is not a bedroom when there is no bed? Wrong. When there is no wardrobe? Wrong. A bedroom is not a bedroom if it is not an upstairs room with an attached bathroom? Wrong again.

A bedroom is not a bedroom unless it has an escapable window accessible to it. The building inspector pointed this out in one of his previous mid-build visits. Unless you could open a window wide enough to climb out of in case of a fire you cannot legally call the room a bedroom. In my home, we were prevented from widening any windows and so one bedroom was left with the original arrow slit style narrow glassed windows. Thin, narrow windows that had originally been simple openings to allow the barn to breath and its contents not to go rotten. For the purposes of fire safety, my home could only ever be described as a two bedroomed home. Anyway back to the main point.

The building inspector from the council was due that morning and as mentioned, he was bang on time – a rarity for anything in the building industry. A full and final visit was needed to commission the barn officially as a home. A fail here meant it was back to the proverbial 'drawing board' and my penfriend at the bank to fix whatever issues had been found.

The building inspector toured the site with myself and the builder. Hard hat, high visibility vest and clipboard at the ready he asked a series of questions. At this point a tip is to show the inspector around as if you are showing a potential home buyer around your property. Keep it positive, hide anything potentially unfavourable out of the way and stay on the positive. Plus keep all your important records in a big box, safely away from the dust, rain and other paper-based accidents you could have on a building site.

"Have you got a certificate to say your electrics are safe and tested?", he enquired.

"Yes, here it is", the builder replied.

The tour continued to the gas boiler under the stairs.

"Have you got your gas fitter's certificate for the boiler?" he asked.

"Yes, here it is". I replied.

"Have you got adequate ventilation for your stove fire?" he asked.

"Yes, here are the ventilation holes and here's the carbon monoxide detector", I replied.

The tour of the home continued and the builder took most of the technical questions. The only concern was the two missing corner brackets that fastened the glass walkway panels to one ninety degree turned, filler glass panel that was to give the whole glass railing its strength.

I slid in front of the building inspector as he searched from room to room for any defects. Then it was time for the walkway and its glass panelled railings. He looked at the glass and rested a good, solid hand on it and pulled. Luckily for me, the building inspector gripped the opposite glass panels and give them a hefty shake. The glass panels remained reassuringly unmovable and he moved on. Phew. I had visions of him shaking my side and watching in terror as the whole thing fell away from the side of the bridge walkway. And then as it hit the floor below, expensively collapsing into millions of pieces. It would still take a month before I had the missing fasteners but today what was in place was almost there. It would hold in place until the job was completed.

Everything around the barn was checked for defects or potential dangers. Even the toilet was flushed in the main bathroom to ensure there was no trickery or likelihood of catching someone literally with their pants down when the toilet was flushed. Lights were switched on and off. Windows were checked in bedrooms to ensure even the largest of escapees could open the wide, hinged windows.

Upon the inspector's return to the ground floor, I knew the inspection was over. He finally took one more look around the living room, reached for his pen and wrote on his clipboard.

"Well done, you've done well. You've passed", he calmly stated.

We shook hands and the inspector made his way out through the kitchen and was gone. Only thirty minutes and he had seen enough to secure his confidence in the barn.

I turned and shook hands with the builder. He'd done a great job and it couldn't have been done without him or his company. He returned the favour by mentioning my head for heights and acrobatics in removing the roof – they couldn't have done it without me. I felt pride, real pride in what we had achieved. But it wasn't time to celebrate fully just yet.

It was time to get married. But not to the builder, to my fiancée. The completion date for occupying the house would race against the date, now set in proverbial stone, of the wedding and its accompanying paraphernalia.

I always thought I'd get married at 30 years old. That's my 'norm referencing' again because most of my friends were getting married around that age. I'd been with my fiancée to countless weddings and we secretly kept mental notes of which weddings were best and which features of the day we copy and use at our wedding. I was thirty-five by the time we were due to head down our own church aisle and be married. My late marriage was not a problem because of 'peer referencing' with my Dad. Dad also got married at thirty-five years old which was old by the standards of the late 1970s. He was also incidentally the same waist measurement as me at thirty-four inches and even the same height at five feet, ten inches and a half despite later shrinking with age In my disaster prone and now increasingly superstitious mind, the numbers alone suggested everything was on track.

The race track had been set. The wedding was going to be a large traditional church service. I had ten groomsmen made up of my closest friends and family. My fiancée had event planned the day with military precision. Chance was out and lists of clear, itemised instructions were in. Each groomsman had a job to perform from a personalised sheet of tasks which also dictated where and when to act. The church was alive with activity and chatter as guests took their places.

A wedding is a huge undertaking on the day itself never mind the year before planning. Services such as champagne reception, vintage hire-car, suit hire, make-up artists and a plethora of other services have to be choreographed for the day from start to finish. Photographers are under even more pressure to deliver the sort of images a proud couple can share and pore over with bored children and then bored grandchildren in minute detail for decades to come.

Eventually, guests seated, the scene was set for the big entrance.

The bride arrived with her very proud father. When the vicar asked "Who gives this bride away to be married", he replied "I do" with the conviction of a loud, firm voice that echoed around the whole church and made my bride literally jump.

The service proceeded like any other wedding. I won't bore you with the details other than the reception at a nearby country home had some great speeches, lots of music, almost endless booze and a hangover from partying that was guaranteed for most. The service did have two ominous incidents however.

According to my superstitious mother, the dropping of the ring by the vicar during the service heralds future dire bad luck. The vicar dropped the ring not once, but twice. At the time I was more concerned that the ring would bounce down one of the nearby grates flanking the main aisle and I'd spend the remainder of the day with a tool box trying to get it out again. The 'ting' sound of the ring bouncing down the stone steps will echo in my memory for eternity. Bad luck would follow but that's for a later chapter. This was a happy day and a day of our closest family and friends coming together to help us celebrate a new life together through great speeches, great hugs and great drinking.

Work continued on the barn in our absence. Smaller tinkering, finishing off the painting, installing the shelving for the walk-in wardrobe and of course the carpet to name but a few of the many smaller tasks left. The carpet worried me as a very relaxed, chilled-out carpet shop owner had taken the measurements. And by now the building budget was depleted so I'd ordered the cheapest, bland creamy-beige, dirt-hiding, inoffensive carpet I could find to match the mahogany and white paintwork. The carpet fitter would be let into the barn and left to his own devices. I'd learnt that a lack of direct and regular supervision led to similar results in the classroom, i.e. things would not get done, there would probably be errors and then fixing the work after the class or carpet fitter had gone would be almost impossible without a lot of suffering.

However, I had no time to lose, after the wedding it was time for the honeymoon. The three cities of Las Vegas, then San Francisco and finally Santa Monica and its conjoined cousin of Las Angeles were the destinations on the itinerary over the coming, fortnight-long honeymoon.

Again, I won't bore you with the details, after all you're here to read about a building project not what I did on honeymoon. The flight was long, very long but just as I'd given up hope of ever using my legs again we arrived in Las Vegas. Highlights? Yep – Las Vegas was an adult playground. You could shoot the sort of weapons only available in the UK to people like the SAS on gun ranges. Targets that were a variation of British singer Amy Winehouse drawn as a drug-fuelled vampire or people from the Middle East holding someone hostage. The Americans were clearly not politically correct and afterwards, if you were American you could also train to carry a gun in public and buy a gun-carrying permit. In the gift shop, Americans could buy a fifty cal. gun powerful enough to shoot bullets at passing aircraft.

Las Vegas was exceptional. You could do anything from gambling, to visiting outrageous clubs and strip clubs, and even get your own butler whilst walking past full scale replicas of world renowned landmarks such as the Statue of Liberty, the Pyramids, volcanos, Venetian canals or the Eiffel Tower! All in the fifty degree heat of a desert! It was a place for walking around star struck and if you watched films like the 'The Hangover' or had seen Britney Spears get married, then every corner you turned you recognised a familiar scene from TV. The city was open twenty-four hours a day, seven days a week. Gamblers could desperately spend their final coins whilst pleading for a miracle or lounge lizards could come back from extravagant shows where you sat in giant chandeliers suspended from the ceiling. Nothing was quiet or impossible.

San Francisco was a much more laid back destination. Apparently one president remarked that the coldest winter he had experienced was a summer spent in San Francisco. He was right. The sea breeze came down the coast from Alaska and it was seriously cold. The 'advanced tickets only' Alcatraz's old civil war fort, cum infamous prison dominated the harbour area with its iconic shape and watch towers. It was partly so hard to escape because the freezing sea surrounding it would kill you in minutes. And that's only if the tide and currents didn't drown you first.

The Golden Gate Bridge was an enormous spectacle. Not actually golden in colour but red from the red oxide used to protect it, it is the first bridge so high up above the sea that aircraft routinely fly under it, not over it! It was vast with the main middle span suspended high above the sea for over a mile between the suspension cable towers. And the streets with trams traversing up and down the hills of San Francisco were everywhere just as they appear in Hollywood films. Simply hop on and off despite the fact that if you did this with a British tram or train you'd be arrested or found in several hundred pieces along a hundred metre stretch of rail. The trams were heavy duty train carriages with wooden benches and worth a ride in the way you'd want to ride in a gondola when visiting Venice.

Los Angeles was the final stop. Muscle Beach where governor for the county – Arnold Schwarzenegger - pumped steel and the beach where the Bay Watch TV babes ran down is located in its beachy neighbour of Santa Monica. For anyone who's waited silently, hoping for their laptop to load anytime soon the Microsoft image of a beach with a bridge over it is the same beach where the Babe, sorry Baywatch, girls and boys roamed.

LA was a sprawling metropolis adjoining luxurious Beverly Hills but also the seedy Hollywood Boulevard walk of Fame. By day, a bristling, mega city where its inhabitants had time for no one, by night a dangerous city of homelessness and vagrancy. Santa Monica is where we stayed – conjoined to LA but separated by a cheap and seemingly endless stream of state run coaches that took thirty minutes in traffic to reach LA. Impressive testament to the size of LA given the coaches were driving only in a straight line to and from Santa Monica and LA. Here the divide between the large BMW-driving wealthy and the luckless masses sleeping rough in LA was stark. Even our hotel owner had a Ferrari parked prominently and conspicuously inside the hotel's underground carpark – just metres from abandoned looking people with their entire lives in shopping trolleys outside.

Santa Monica had an amazing beach. You could understand why the thousands of miles of Route 66 finished at the Santa Monica Pier. It was a perfect, well presented holiday maker's beach. Wide, open, perfect sands for relaxing or sun worshipping with paths for Fitbit clad joggers and roller-skating, bikini girls. The beach was also a safe haven despite what lay out-side Santa Monica in Los Angeles. The life guards protected the sandy beaches and surf, LA police helicopters patrolled the skies and the coast guard motor launches watched the sea.

166

After LA and Santa Monica, it was time to return home. But unlike most newly-weds, we'd be going to separate beds and separate homes. Why? We hadn't fallen out and certainly hadn't had enough of each other's company even though we'd spent most of the pre-wedding days tied up with our separate wedding and building projects. It felt strange to drop your wife and her luggage back off at her parents and return home alone. There was a quietness after the hectic pace of the wedding and especially after the desperate rush to finish building before running off to sight-see everything possible in our short visit to some of America's most famous cities. Things were suddenly very quiet.

The barn delays and overly optimistic race against time to complete our wedding, go on our honeymoon and build the remaining things had meant that unless we wanted to camp on the floor it was time to make a much needed effort to furnish the barn. In furniture terms, we needed everything and anything, and especially a bed for two.

Despite the mounting debts, some issues with credit cards and the lack of funds it was time to take our shoestring budget and stretch it even further. Even further than a small child's excuse for getting caught, red-handed in a chocolate box meant for someone else's birthday. It was time to furnish the empty spaces of our home to be. It was time to go furniture shopping.

Chapter 17 – The Challenges of No Furniture

"The only really good place to buy lumber is at a store where the lumber has already been cut and attached together in the form of furniture finished and put inside boxes".

Dave Barry, 'The Taming of the Screw: How to Sidestep Several Million Homeowner's Problems.'

One of the most pleasant memories I have as a child is waking up in my own bed on a summer's morning during the school holidays, knowing I didn't need to get out of bed for school, and being able to relax in the most comfy place I'd ever known - the bed I had grown up with. Familiar and comfortable. Like all of my bedroom furniture right down to the superman lampshade, everything was familiar and comfortable but ultimately chosen by me as a small child.

The situation was now different, I'd no longer be relying on the single man's stock of furniture. That furniture stock for most men living with their parents is pretty much nothing. Even during my time away, as a manager of a Toys R Us store I never owned my own furniture because I was always on the move from city to city, living in furnished hotels. I never seemed to get round to buying furniture even when I moved back home to train as a teacher. The closest I got to buying furniture was a big wide screen TV. It simply wasn't a priority or necessity – until now.

I wasn't alone. My fiancée, now wife, was in an equally furniture-neglecting situation while living at her family home. She owned a TV and a chair bringing our total furniture count to two TVs and a chair. It was looking like the overall rustic design of the building was going to be replaced by the minimalist look instead. It was time for furniture shopping and canvassing relatives for any unwanted pieces of furniture.

Furniture was now something for the first time in our lives that we needed to tackle. We needed to become fully seasoned adults with our very own stock of furniture. We needed everything but at least we could choose the furniture between us and furnish our new home together like a 'real' couple. Smaller items such as mixers, toasters and kettles etc...had been happily supplied in abundance as wedding gifts. In theory, with the new kitchen and its fitted ovens, we could at least feed ourselves even if we had to eat off plates resting on the kitchen floor. It was time to sort out the big things such as sofas to sit on and a bed to sleep in.

Some things were easier to sort out than others. For example, somewhere to sleep came quickly from Marks and Spencer's furniture outlet thanks to collecting a lot of wedding vouchers together and spending the lot on one big purchase of a king-sized bed. After trying a range of mattresses from a bewildering array of styles and materials I knew nothing about, we finally settled on a bed and mattress. It was a combination that approximated to the warm, comfortable and familiar bed I had possessed as a child.

Everything was needed. After a few weeks of living like squatters on tins of food and eating from plates in our laps in the kitchen it was time for kitchen furniture. A kitchen table was essential to avoid wearing our meal spillages. A table came second hand but quickly from an uncle and although it didn't match any planned décor, a kitchen table and chairs was a very utilitarian and useful starting point.

It's amazing what you take for granted. For example, trying to keep our milk fresh for a couple of days was difficult because we didn't have a fridge. And nothing lasts a shorter period of time than milk and dairy products in the summer when they are not being refrigerated. The novelty of collecting milk with a jug your dad's given you and plunging it into the farm's milk tank each day then walking home come rain or shine rapidly wears off. It's also an eye opener to look at all the food that does actually need to belong in a fridge. Unless you're storing bread and tins of beans like some sort of 'end of world is coming' nut job, most things belong in the fridge. Luckily retailers such as Comet deliver fridges for ten pounds. More importantly they price matched anyone, including stores on the internet, which profit-wise is probably the reason why they don't exist anymore.

Other things such as sofas were a bit more of a challenge. Flat pack furniture would become the bane of my life. Fiddley bolts or ambiguous plans that didn't match any part of a sofa or set of drawers were the norm. At times, we struggled to haul into the house and upstairs ready-made furniture we begged and borrowed from family and friends.

However, this was the barn and things were never going be straightforward. The wonderful people at the flat-pack furniture retail-giant store would prove how difficult you can truly make things if you try.

Following a visit to the flat-pack furniture retail-giant it was suggested that it would be a great idea to get one of the brand new sofas that converted into a bed for visitors to stay over, but looked like a great farmhouse style sofa when you weren't expecting guests.

With my wife now expecting a baby I needed to get a move on. As I told you before, I always end up in a continuous mad dash from one project to another at break-neck speed. My wife was expecting a baby and a fold out sofa would be great for my wife's mum to stay over. My wife's mum would be able to support her in the early days after the baby's arrival and after I had gone back to work.

We had seen a sofa bed. We had asked the staff to mock the sofa bed up on a computer in various different colours and we settled for something that matched the barn's paintwork. The sofa also matched the by now fitted carpets and the rustic feel of the barn. Unfortunately we were in my car which was a small two seater sports car - I know I can hear the hairdresser jokes coming - so we needed the sofa bed delivering. The staff took payment, my address details and promised the sofa bed would be with us by the end of the week.

The sales staff at the flat-pack furniture retail giant said that the driver would text when he was ten minutes away from our home. And the driver did text us to alert us to his impending visit.

Being paranoid and having access to CCTV, I switched on the monitor to my own grandstand view, courtesy of my new closed circuit television system. On my monitor, I watched the camera over the shared driveway and sure enough the furniture delivery van started reversing up the shared driveway another small, sturdy body joined the scene. Mrs Interfering was on hand as usual and now trying to tell the driver to go away.

I left my monitor and ran out of the barn and over to the delivery truck. I could hear Mrs Interfering tell the driver that my address didn't exist and that he should leave or she'd call the police. I told the driver to ignore the dear old neighbour. My address did exist, he was at the right place to drop off the furniture.

The delivery driver was bemused by the greeting he was receiving but he was very helpful. The driver ignored Mrs Interfering and helped me carry the boxes into the barn. I signed his electronic PDA to say that I had received the delivery and within minutes he was gone.

This is where I made a crucial mistake. Excitedly, I opened all the boxes and pulled out all of the contents. With my tool box open and ready I noticed there was a problem. There wasn't half as much metal work and wooden pieces as I had expected. When I Googled the flat-pack furniture retail-giant's website I realised that I should have received four boxes and not three. I was missing a large box of parts. I assumed that the missing box was probably still on the delivery truck and as I had the driver's mobile phone number, I phoned him.

"I'm missing some boxes", I desperately stated.

"Sorry mate, there's nothing left on board. I'll give you the number for the warehouse. You can check if the missing box is there and then we'll deliver it", the driver replied.

He gave me the warehouse depot number and I rang them. After a wait, a polite lady answered and said they would look for the missing box and ring me back.

A day later the lady still hadn't rung back, so I rang again and got a similar message. The staff would have a look and then give me a call back.

I rang the warehouse number each day for days until I decided to ring customer services. Customer services then said they would have a look and then get the warehouse staff to give me a call back.

The staff didn't call back. I rang customer services a number of times, each time I was on hold from anywhere between 10 minutes to half an hour. Each time I got a different person with a different phone number. When you rang each phone number back you got the main switchboard options instead. The switchboard options then subdivided into some more options, which themselves subdivided into even more options. These options again divided into more options. Contacting a specific employee was like searching for a needle in a haystack task. Email proved no more effective either. My emails were followed by automatically generated emails from the company's computer. Contact by technology was impossible. Carrier pigeon, flares and even a personal journey to their distribution centre crossed my mind.

It was time for belligerent Dave to come out. Skills honed to perfection over the previous year of chasing wayward suppliers were going to be put to good use. I realised from my research that if I put a Small Claims Court application in, the company could no longer ignore me. They would either have to send me the missing parts or refund me. Better still, I also realised that I could charge the supplier expenses to cover all the time and effort I had wasted. I could bill the enemy firm with 'reasonable' costs such as telephone costs thanks to a law designed to stop utility companies from wilfully ignoring their customers.

I logged on to the government's Small Claims Court website. Luckily, the flat-pack furniture retail-giant was using a UK-based website. The website and headquarters of the company were based in England which meant I could pursue them through the Small Claims Court. Unlike Scottish Power who would later dodge me for months using Scottish law and the less intuitive, Sheriff's office. Instead, in England, I filled in my details and submitted my fee of two hundred pounds to lodge the claim. I told the Small Claims Court what my claim was for and pressed the 'Submit Claim' button.

The effect was almost immediate. The flat-pack furniture retail giant received a copy of the letter in the post within a few days. And this time a minion didn't ring up with vague fob offs and leave telephone numbers that to all intents and purposes were useless. Instead, I got the UK and Ireland Customer Services Manager – finally someone paid to care and in a position of power. I was finally way above the minions and their comedy of switchboard errors and generic email advice.

The UK and Ireland Customer Services Manager blamed the new computer system for not tracking customer complaints more accurately. He apologised for the inconvenience caused. A full refund, plus money to cover my costs and my time were in my bank within a few days. After months of hunting I at least had my money back.

I asked him about the parts of the furniture they had already delivered. What did he want doing with the three boxes of parts? The manager briefly thought and then said I should dispose of the pieces in whatever way was most convenient to me. Straightaway I thought about matches. I'd been burning quite a lot of mess and building waste. Anything I wasn't legally allowed to burn such as polluting plastics, I was taking away to skips and the local council. This furniture was wood however. It was going to be triumphantly burned.

To celebrate my victory of David versus Goliath battle I had a plan. I had won against the flat-pack furniture retail giant and organised a much needed celebration. I got my wife and a couple of her friends who were visiting to watch a bonfire. I had carefully prepared a stack of rubbish with the furniture at the centre. I stacked up the wooden pieces and put some paper at the bottom and added the matches.

Whoosh! I was almost part of the fire! The flammable nature of the furniture was phenomenal!! No sooner had I added the matches and fiddled around with the burning newspaper, the furniture spectacularly burst into flames. The size of the fire was enormous and spread rapidly. The fire was eye catching. I have a great picture of the neighbours coming out to see what this early bonfire was doing in mid-summer. They couldn't believe that I hadn't thrown any petrol on the fire!

I learnt a few valuable lessons about courts and fires. The first was to get to delivery drivers before the neighbours did. That avoided any 'emotional fires'. The second, to check carefully anything that gets delivered to make sure you have everything before the driver vanishes. The third lesson is, that if you want a victory against carefree, faceless corporations, use the Small Claims Court for fast results. Unless you're based in Scotland and then it's the Sheriff's Office which is a much fiddlier ordeal. And fourthly, no-one, under any circumstances, sits on any of my remaining flat-pack furniture smoking.

174

Chapter 18 – New Builds Always Have Teething Troubles

"Most new build homes have some sort of initial teething problems. The Consumer Code For Home Builders applies to home buyers who, on or after 1 April 2010, bought a new or newly converted home built by a home builder registered and insured by one of the following home warranty bodies; National House Building Council, Premier Guarantee and LABC Warranty. The Code's pre-sale and handover requirements apply to home buyers who are the first purchasers of that particular home. The Code's after-sales service applies to anyone who was the initial purchaser of the home but also to any subsequent buyers of that home within the first two years of the initial purchase. The Consumer Code for Home Builders is an industry-led code of conduct for builders, which was developed to make the home buying process fairer and more transparent for purchasers".

Adapted from Which? Consumer Magazine 2018

A friend of mine bought a brand new, shiny house on a new estate. All of the houses were built in the last three years and initially looked amazing. However a few years later and their newness hasn't stopped some of them developing bows in their walls. Some have been built with bricks that are not even level. Instead, each row of bricks forms a wavy pattern up and down the external walls of some unfortunate home owners. Some of the new build home owners have additional features such as bendy roofs or chimneys that move in the wind. Some have gardens made of topsoil thinly coating heavy layers of clay. The clay is so compacted that rain water doesn't drain away and instead the extra water creates green, stagnant ponds.

As a self-builder, you are the architect of your own brilliance but also your own misery. If you do something half-hearted it's not going to be a faceless stranger that picks up the mess and the bill to fix it. You have to put it right. No scrimping on the pain or missing that tight corner join on a pipe. 'Fix things' and 'do things properly' should be your building motto.

You are also the architect of your own brilliance and the reward for adding years of grey hair and stress to your life comes from many different places. It could be the amazing view you get by positioning the windows to overlook a beautiful valley. Or it could be the VAT. What? I hear you cry, VAT?! Yes, as a self-builder, you can claim VAT back as a new builder now building for yourself. You've spent VAT on pretty much everything and you can claim it back. At last a nest egg to replace all those bank statements with minus symbols at the start of each number! Another source of money for fixing things are building guarantees.

Pretty much all buildings built in this day and age are covered by a minimum, ten year guarantee. Despite the complexity of a house, the buildings are generally far more reliable than the electrical devices that many people put inside them. A big tip is, however, to keep yet another big box of receipts, guarantees, certificates and warranties, as you'll never quite know when you need them. Always check the documents that come with equipment because a lot of items require you to provide some input. Many devices need you to actually activate the guarantee by giving away your address and details on a freepost postcard back to the manufacturer.

I was lucky with my builder. Having a builder live next door has some advantages for me and disadvantages for him. On one occasion, my wife created an indoor waterfall; every time she had a bath in the main bathroom, she'd pull the plug and water would pour out through the ceiling below. The water poured from her bath and into the hallway where we stored our coats and shoes. Soggy shoes on a crisp September morning are definitely a great way to ruin the start to a new school term. The squelching and the cold was miserable.

It turns out the cause of the misery was a missing seal on the pipe taking the waste water away from the bath. When the plug was pulled, water raced down the wrong side of the pipe and through the flooring and plasterboard below. The builder fixed these without complaint.

Another issue was with a gap between the handmade window frames in the bedroom. As the air got cooler outside, the frames and the rubber seals started to shrink and made a small gap where the wind could pass freely through. The builder soon sorted this out. We were again airtight and insulated against the increasingly cold autumnal weather.

What he couldn't fix however was our meddling neighbour. For the old dear everything from the postman to visitors was fair game. Post started going missing which was worrying especially as I still had penfriends at the bank. CCTV provided an answer as I saw Mrs Interfering bullying the postman on a number of occasions. The postman said she threatened to sue him for coming up the shared drive to deliver our post.

The post service is unique in the United Kingdom. I found out from ringing our legal advice line that the postman is a unique individual under the law. Historically, the postman has a charter to deliver the Queen's taxes and beyond a member of the police, he or she is one of the few people who can go anywhere in the name of his or her job. Most importantly a postman or woman is protected by the law.

It is also a criminal offence to stop the postman or interfere with the post. I spoke to Mrs Interfering and the postman about this. I even moved our post box so that the postman didn't have to walk as far to get to us. In my cost-cutting efforts I'd gone for a new plastic, lightweight post box. And I nailed it to my gate post. Unfortunately, the new post box fell off and was blown by the wind onto the shared drive. Mrs Interfering misses nothing and I have a great video of her doing a three-point turn over the top of the post box with her car.

Ironically Mrs Interfering liked to turn delivery person herself. Regularly, I could see her on the motion triggered CCTV images using our garden as a dustbin. The alarm would go off and as I switched our TV to the CCTV camera feeds you could see Mrs Interfering empty her bins into my garden. She was no fan of dogs either. I caught her throwing things over into my garden designed to create a trip to the vet.

Mrs Interfering was a huge teething problem for the new build and her sons were no better. The youngest son could see this was all going to end up in court. So one day after arguing with each other over some trivia, we agreed to swap phone numbers and discuss solutions to problems rather than indulge in continued bickering. The overall promise was if his mother didn't do anything to us, we in return would ignore her. This was a great agreement and kept my wife happy too.

It wasn't to last very long. In fact, you could count the hours the cease fire held. Like a cease fire in the Middle East, the bombs were poised for any excuse to set them off again. The trigger mechanism came in the form of a wandering BT telephone engineer.

The following day and day two of the cease fire, the telephone engineer had got lost. He'd come up the contested Gaza strip of the shared drive despite my instructions to the contrary. The engineer was here to fix a problem we had with the broadband. Unfortunately I could hear the youngest son was telling the engineer that our address didn't exist. The engineer looked understandably confused when he could see my house number bolted to my gate. He could see the barn to and just needed to go behind Mrs Interfering's son and through the gate to start his work. Mrs Interfering's son smiled when I ran out to stop the engineer driving off. He had been rumbled breaking his own ceasefire agreement and he laughed.

The same son would go on to break quite a lot of ceasefire agreements.

By now the barn was almost very nearly completed except for a fence which should have been erected around the edge of my property before we moved in. The fencing was a technicality I had forgotten about and which my wife enjoyed. You could literally reach out of a window and stroke a passing cow. One cow, one day, even lovingly rubbed it's mucky behind all over a window whilst we were eating tea. Passing sheep would come and look through the windows to see what their human neighbours were watching on TV. For a town girl not used to this close proximity to nature, the absence of a fence was not a problem. My wife used to love seeing nature up close more than ever before.

However we had problems. We were technically not meant to be occupying the house on a technicality. The wire sheep fence hadn't been put up by this time and it should have been. The planning permission terms were reconsidered thanks to the neighbours' meddling. Right before our occupation, even though the house was completely liveable, the new terms stated; *"a fence shall be erected around the curtilage of the property..."* The busy start of a new school term meant both of us as teachers were back at work, running our lives at a hundred miles an hour and had failed to notice the technicality.

The neighbours had noticed. They were not happy about this breach of planning terms and had indeed studied every last intricacy and technicality of our home. People would visit the house and its grounds anonymously. They would take samples of the garden, the drive and walls. Others would take photographs. Whilst having my tea, I'd see the flash of a camera or mobile phone. On the CCTV, which wasn't public knowledge that we had this yet, we would see people walking around the grounds of the house as if appointed by some law enforcement agency to check up on us.

I'd had enough of these intrusions into my private life. After all, I wasn't a celebrity and I wasn't a footballer. Stalking me was clearly ridiculous and even concerning as the dark nights of winter drew in.

We called the police who spoke to the neighbours about not coming on to our property uninvited. This didn't stop the youngest son however. My wife became very nervous of the situation. My mum became concerned too. She even bought us curtains for the barn so intruders could not see in.

Intruders to the barn's grounds were the least of my worries. As things escalated with the neighbours, tempers would flare out of control.

One day I came home after a busy day to find an alarm going off on one of my CCTV cameras. When I replayed the camera footage, to my horror I found that the youngest son had been videoed chasing my elderly father away from my home. The last footage from the camera was just before the neighbour's youngest son ripped out the camera from its wall fixture. It was after man-handling my elderly Dad and then chasing him back to his home. How this ended I had no idea as the camera system was now damaged.

Things were escalating out of control. It was time to call the police again. Things were getting beyond the teething troubles of a new house. Things were getting to the point where doors would be locked at all times to make sure that no one came in or near my wife. My wife by this time was wondering what on earth she had got herself into living here.

I spoke to my family about what had been seen on the CCTV. My Dad had gone to investigate someone moving around near the barn. He knew my wife and I would still be at work. Given the history and the issues of the barn my Dad had gone to investigate. We all agreed what happened next was unacceptable and it was time for the police to intervene.

When you ring 999, the line gets answered very quickly. You are then given three options - do you want an ambulance, the fire brigade or the police? Once you choose the police, a dispatcher asks you for your details and then uses a series of questions to determine how urgent the call is.

In my Dad's case the incident had come and it had gone. My dad had been pushed and chased back to his bungalow some metres away from my barn. He'd been threatened but then the attacker was gone. The perpetrator was no longer around and as we knew who the attacker was, there would be a wait until a police officer became free to take a statement from my Dad.

We waited for about an hour for a police officer to arrive at my brother's farmhouse nearby, further away from the barn. Eventually, there was a knock at the farmhouse door. An officer arrived and in he came. He was a young officer but tall and broad built. He took his peaked hat off, sat down and listen with his notepad in his hand.

My Dad retold the story of what had happened but the video footage said it all. My Dad had been assaulted. He had been chased for his life until a laughing pursuer, Mrs Interfering's son, decided he had had his fun.

The police officer said he would go and interview Mrs Interfering's son about the incident and report back after his next shift. He left a crime reference number made up of the day's date and a unique incident number, in case we needed to contact the police again in the meantime.

The officer left and we discussed what happened again. Dad was brave but we knew it had shaken him up. He sat quietly as we talked over the problem. The manhandling and chase would have been enough to shake anyone of us up.

I was just beginning to believe the barn was jinxed and needed a priest, a four leaf clover, a lucky horseshoe or whatever, to stem the regular issues that seemed to plague the barn.

Suddenly my phone went. It was my wife asking when I would be back up at the barn. She was only a hundred metres away but I could hear the trembling in her voice. Something had happened or was happening. She needed me now, urgently.

I raced, headlong into yet another life experience. In fact I'd raced into a trap. I raced into a trap that would lead to me being interviewed in the local police station. The trap would lead to a formal police station interview. This chapter was going to involve a new experience and a whole new, learning curve. I was about to experience barn teething troubles of a different kind.

Chapter 19 – A Police Station And A Baby

"You have the right to free legal advice (legal aid) if you're questioned at a British police station. You can change your mind later if you turn it down. You must be told about your right to free legal advice after you're arrested and before you're questioned at a police station, you can:

1 - Ask for the police station's 'duty solicitor' - they're available 24 hours a day and independent of the police

2 - Tell the police you would like legal advice - the police will contact the Defence Solicitor Call Centre (DSCC)

3 - Ask the police to contact a solicitor, e.g. your own solicitor.

You may be offered legal advice over the phone instead of a duty solicitor if you're suspected of having committed a less serious offence, e.g. being disorderly. The advice is free and independent of the police.

Once you've asked for legal advice, the police can't question you until you've got it - with some exceptions. The police can make you wait for legal advice in serious cases, but only if a senior officer agrees. The longest you can be made to wait before getting legal advice is 36 hours after arriving at the police station (or 48 hours for suspected terrorism)."

Adapted from 'Your Rights on Being Arrested', www.gov.uk 2017.

For most people, the inside of a police station is a mystery and few will have seen the inside of a police station beyond what they have seen on TV. For those who do visit a police station it's most likely they will never get past the front desk as they report a minor nuisance, missing family pet or show their driving documents after a routine vehicle check.

For me however, I was going to get the 'full tour'. The attack on my Dad had been reported to the police. The police would now go and find the perpetrator - the neighbours' son - and begin their interview with him.

In the meantime there was another problem. A hasty call from my worried wife confirmed there was still somebody in the area. The person had been banging on the door of the barn and my wife was afraid to answer it. This person was now Mrs Interfering's other, older son. We had heard that the older son had a reputation for aggression. As my brother and I reached the barn we looked around in the dark and eventually towards the lighting of the contested, shared drive, we saw a figure. It was the figure of Mrs Interfering's older son. He was leaning against his car across the shared access and staring at us. He was a tall individual at around six feet, three inches or more. He was in a black puffer jacket, the padded jacket increasing his bulk under the nearby house lights. He was now glaring at us.

We approached the menacing individual, aware that somewhere in the dark night and shadows the other brother could be lurking. Angry words were exchanged. Accusations were fired in the air. Mrs Interfering came out and joined her son. They argued with us about who had caused our families to be at loggerheads.

A ten minute, verbal battle raged with tempers flaring. Lights from nearby houses quickly switched on as the shouting continued. The normally quiet neighbourhood reverberated to the noise of hate and anger.

Both sides eventually shouted each other to a standstill. And, almost as if the fire was running out of fuel, the shouting subsided. Both sides left to lick their verbal wounds.

Unfortunately our wounds were greater. We had been trapped.

Mrs Interfering's younger son on the day of assaulting my Dad had destroyed a vital CCTV camera. He'd wrenched it from a fixture on a wall near the barn before continuing to chase my dad. The camera damage was more than simply putting one camera out of action.

The ripping out of the camera by its wire interrupted the power to the recording box. The camera had been powered by a wire that ran back to the barn and then it entered through a small pipe opening. In the pipe, the wire that held both power to the camera and transmitted data back to the DVR recorder was vulnerable. The aggressive wrenching of the camera's wire had then damaged the recording box. Today there would be no digital eye witnesses to keep us safe. Wires for another camera overlooking the flared tempers no longer mattered. The recording box was out of action. The rear of the recording box with its delicate hard disk drive was forced open. The screwed in camera connector had been pulled with force beyond its design. In essence the safe-guarding, digital eyes that saw and recorded everything were blind. Nothing since the vandalism earlier in the day had been recorded by the box including this event. This blindness was going to cost us dear.

I should have known something would happen, like a tin of beans in a microwave, an obvious explosion was moments away. Mrs Interfering had ramped up the number of calls to the police about anything and everything she could think of. Our solicitor stated very clearly that the reason for all the calls to the police were for one thing and one thing only. Each time the police are called out, a simple entry is made under a crime reference number. No judgement is made as to whether the call is for authentic reasons or not. No judgement is made unless the police carry out an investigation. The crime number simply has the caller's concern noted under it. However, Mrs Interfering was not calling the police randomly. She was purposefully adding to a list under the number.

Most importantly, a crime reference number and the list of entries made on it can be accessed. Details of dates of when the calls were made and what the caller said happened can be requested from the police and used as supporting evidence for a civil action. In our solicitor's opinion, Mrs Interfering was no longer calling the police randomly but building up the case for a civil lawsuit in the absence of an official, police prosecution.

And a big ramp up was coming in response to our assault claim against her son. Two days after the arguments with Mrs Interfering and her son, a local neighbourhood policing officer phoned. She asked myself and for my brother to come to Clitheroe police station as soon as possible. Mrs Interfering's son was requesting the police to prosecute us for an alleged assault. The alleged assault was when we had met the older son, just a day after the younger son assaulted my dad. Without camera footage of what really happened we were in trouble. We were also informed by the neighbourhood officer that we could either turn up of our own voluntary accord or be arrested.

The instruction to attend a police station was devastating. All manner of accusations and allegations ran through my mind and my brother's mind. Anything could have been said and made up, especially as our CCTV was now a mass of blank screens and corrupted data.

The police suggested a mediation session should be set up by the police at a neutral venue between our two families. This could solve the circus of allegations and counter allegations. The police rightly saw the continuing hostilities as ultimately unhelpful. And more importantly, on the verge of seeing someone being charged and their life being permanently ruined.

The officer said that the Interfering's family would drop their assault accusation against us if we dropped our assault claim in return. My dad was shaken up and I sensed a negotiation with 'terrorists' was coming. As Margaret Thatcher said during the 1982 Iranian Embassy siege in London; if you negotiate with terrorists you'll soon encourage more bombs. She sent the SAS in and shot their hostages' way to freedom. We didn't have access to the SAS but Thatcher's sentiment sort of made sense. I also thought about Winston Churchill. Churchill likened negotiating a forced truce with Hitler during World War II to be like trying to negotiate with a lion when your head is in its mouth. When speaking to Parliament, Churchill urged everyone to remain strong and determined not to surrender. We would not be dropping our assault claim and in fright, feebly walk away. I would stand my ground for my home.

The police next recommended mediation. Both sides would sit down and under police supervision would sort out their differences and resolve the on going battle. If the Interferings didn't attend, then the police would continue their assault charge of Mrs Interfering's son.

We agreed to attend mediation if the Interfering boys did and of course more importantly, the lady who started it all - Mrs Interfering. Mrs Interfering's boys agreed to attend mediation but Mrs Interfering flatly refused. We knew without Mrs Interfering the mediation would be a waste of time. However, if we failed to reach agreement about mediation, we'd all be interviewed about each other's assault claim.

Mediation was unacceptable to Mrs Interfering. Out of the whole group of us, she would again get things her own way and declare mediation a non-starter. It would now be a trip to the police station instead. Potentially some of us could be staying there for one or more nights.

As I mentioned earlier, it turns out that when you are interviewed by the police at a police station you have the right to a solicitor - just like on TV. During the first session of the interview with a police officer it is recommended that you choose to have legal representation. Better still, you can be accompanied by solicitor of your choosing which is then paid for by the state and therefore free. Free fitted my budget well.

I rang our solicitor and he was initially stunned by where I was. I was then stunned when he said he didn't specialise in what I was facing. Instead, he recommended a local law firm specialising in all the really bad things in the arena of crime such as assault, murder and more. I was surprised but also impressed that the law practice maintained a twenty-four hours a day, seven days a week police station 'vigil' to help people like me. The law firm had rota of solicitors who can attend at any time to support and advise you. My brother and I arranged a solicitor from the law firm to meet us outside the police station an hour before the police interview.

The criminal law solicitor arrived, as planned, an hour before the interview. She introduced herself to us. We didn't really know what to say to the solicitor because we didn't know what we stood accused of. The only clues was a seemingly odd, out-of-place word that the police officer had used. It was the 'arrest able' sounding word - assault. Our solicitor gave a brief two minute explanation of what to expect.

Her briefing was precise, almost as if she had said it so many times from going through a very familiar routine. The solicitor also said she would speak for us if needed but advised us both 'just to tell the truth and be honest'. We gratefully shook her hand and nervously followed her into the police station to meet our fate.

Unnervingly the interview room was at the back of the police station, just past the almost mediaeval looking iron-barred cages of the police holding cells. The cells were empty but nervously I wondered if I was going to be occupying one of these cages depending on what allegation I was going to be facing.

I've seen Police TV programmes many, many times showing the interview rooms. The interview rooms are usually a drab shade of grey with a school style table in the middle. Then you have plastic chairs one side for the police officers and at the other side for the suspect plus legal advisor. This interview room didn't fail to meet that expectation. The room looked the same as what you'd expect on TV, right down to the old fashioned tape deck used to record statements. What they don't do now though is use the tape deck sitting on the table. Instead they used microphones buried into the ceiling tiles and a simple button to stop and start the recordings. The tape deck was a sort of odd decoration to spruce up an otherwise dull room.

The dull interview room also held a solitary, hefty book. I'd not seen this literary work of art before but it was our 'Book of Rights'. From the phrase 'book 'em' in Police crime dramas, I guessed this was the book that inspired that phrase. The police officer handed me the book, it was the size of a Bible. It looked like it had as many pages as the Bible too. I didn't know if the police officer was serious but she asked if I wanted to read my 'rights'. I looked at my solicitor and she advised along the lines – 'it would take a very long time. Let's do the interview instead'.

The police officer began to introduce the interview in a very formal way. I was warned about lying under oath and reminded of the need to tell the truth. What I said could be used in court against me.

Finally, after two days of worrying I was going to find out what the allegation of assault was about.

The officer asked if I knew the person who had made the accusation. I said I did. She then asked did I see the person on the night in question?

I said I did. As the questioning started to dial in on more specific details, I felt more and more uneasy.

Details of the night raced through my mind and then started to jumble themselves up. I felt guilty even though I knew was innocent. I even started to think that I'm looking guilty to the police officer. I started to think even my solicitor was starting to think I was guilty. Before the police officer could overwhelm me anymore, she pushed an A4 picture that Mrs Interfering's son had taken of his ear. I pulled the image closer to look at what I had allegedly done. Or we had allegedly done, or at least someone had done.

I breathed a massive sigh of relief. My heart started to slow to a manageable rhythm again. Our accuser had a tiny, tiny amount of blood coming from his ear. It could have been described as a shaving cut.

The police officer looked at me and saw my change in temperament. At last I felt comfy or at least comfier again. The son had a minor injury. Whatever the cause it was definitely nothing to do with us. We certainly never hit him in the ears as claimed. The image was laughable but thank goodness it was so poor and something more convincing hadn't been made up. I half-feared some extreme injury was about to appear. An injury like those created by make-up artists in some Hollywood slasher film.

I was relieved and so was my brother. I only hoped that in a vengeful way, Mrs Interfering's son had to face the same upset, anguish and anxiety that we had faced. I hope he squirmed as the police questioned him about my Dad's assault. His questioning ordeal, however, would be multiplied by far more stress due to the video of the very real assault my Dad had faced.

We said a heartfelt thank you to our solicitor before leaving the police station. I don't know if it was the usual experience, some unseen foresight on her behalf or just generally looking for business but the solicitor handed me her card. It was a more durable plastic card with her details "for when if you ever get arrested again" she said. I think she had us confused with real hooligans. Strangely I'd survived this ordeal and though still shaking like a leaf, I suddenly felt like a badass rebel. I'd survived a police interrogation and was a free man! However a quiet voice inside my head told me there's no way I could go into criminality if this is what would happen every time the police took me away for questioning. The experience was one to tell the boys with an added bravado in the pub but not an experience I wanted to reproduce again.

I returned home to my barn. My family where waiting with my wife. With tears in her eyes my wife gave me a big hug. We put the coffee on as myself and my brother relayed the police station interview story to the family.

I could see the stress that all this confrontation was having on my wife. She was naturally a very conscientious person who thought deeply about a lot of things. Although she was a teacher she was naturally very shy. She was no fool and indeed when she was a pupil at secondary school she achieved the highest score for GCSE English in her entire year group. She had mulled over a lot in her head and she was literally shaking. I could tell that the battle with the neighbours and not knowing whether she would run into them each night after coming home from work was getting to her. There wasn't a moment's peace as either council enforcement officers received a 'complaint' about us, or the police were coming round. The trouble was almost weekly and now every few days.

It would only be a short four months before I realised the real toll living in the barn was having on my wife. She didn't feel safe at home and despite buying a pet dog to lift her moods and act as security for her, things were about to take a complete nosedive.

We were going to have a baby. And having a baby was going to create a lot of stress for the average couple, in the average home in the average quiet street. This wasn't the average home or even the average street.

We both looked forward to having a small child, and dreamt about a little him or her wandering around the garden. We dreamed about pushing the pram with the dog alongside and going out for family walks. We both wanted children and if you looked at our friends many of them had already started families. They were now on raising their second child.

We started antenatal sessions as we got closer to the big day. Guests at the sessions were made up of an unusual mixture of people. There were happy and excited parents to be, as well as younger parents who were not intending to start a family but were now expecting a baby whether they liked it or not. In the latter case, I felt sorry for one particular young mum. In the paired activities her feckless boyfriend never took part. She often did the role play and exercises in changing nappies on a doll or feeding the doll on her own. Her indifferent and feckless boyfriend stayed glued to his iPhone. I often wondered if he'd Google what to do when his baby came along and what the consequences would be if there was no phone signal. The antenatal classes were informative and too valuable in my opinion to waste.

You can pay to attend antenatal classes from the RSPCC. Or go for free to NHS classes. We chose the free, once a week sessions at 7 p.m. till 9 p.m. My wife knew the midwife. The midwife leading the sessions was larger than life. She was a very seasoned midwife who had a great way of explaining and humouring away the big baby iceberg that was about to land on each of us. Especially the dreaded pain of labour. Eventually, talk of labour would be replaced by actual labour.

My wife's labour was like most wives' labour - very painful. Her labour lasted hour upon hour over two days. I was impressed with my wife's ability to keep going. But unfortunately the ability to keep going was not going to be enough. Complications arose which threatened her life and also the life of the baby. Just to add another level of complexity, my wife just disclosed her wishes regarding blood transfusions.

This put the midwives and surgeons in a quandary. By the end of the labour, my wife's temperature was skyrocketing and the baby's heartbeat was starting to reach for the sky. Helplessly I was looking at potentially losing both my wife and child.

In the early hours of the next day, doctors rushed my wife into the delivery theatre. Surgeons began to try and get the little baby out. We had now been in hospital for over thirty hours. The question was how do you get a stuck baby out of a mother without cutting her open and performing the usual remedy to a 'baby jam' or breached birth - a blood demanding, caesarean operation?

Sweat poured off the surgeons and mother to be. All manner of methods were tried in the vain hope they would not need to perform an operation.

Eventually the panic was over. A little cry was heard and out popped a healthy baby girl, straight into the hands of the surgeon. Straightaway the little girl was taken to be inspected, weighed and tagged with the name of her mother. When she returned and I held her for the first time, I felt an odd sensation of calm and love. I hadn't felt calm for over a year, or indeed relaxed. I showed my wife our new baby and she smiled, relieved that the baby was here and looking well.

For medical reasons that I won't go into now and should be lost in the mists of time the pregnancy had been a very difficult time for us as a couple. Now, however, we were blessed with a beautiful little girl with the bluest eyes I'd ever seen and it was time to celebrate. I went to the nearest toy shop and picked up a big teddy bear. I settled on a special teddy that could play lullabies. Then I went off to collect grandparents from both mine and my wife's family.

It would soon be time to name our little girl and bring her home with her mummy to a family home. The little baby would join us as a fourth generation of the family to live on the farm.

I had the bunting and flags out ready for the arrival of our tiny bundle of joy. Her little face suggested she was more interested in sleep and my little daughter hasn't changed much since her baby days. She still loves to stay up late and has to be carried to bed. And she certainly does not like early mornings. Early mornings to my little daughter are usually met by the same face you'd expect a vampire to make when seeing the morning sun come up over the horizon. A grimace on a cute little face and a quick duck under her bed covers.

It was truly an amazing time! Milestone wise, we built a house in one year and got married. In the second year, we finished off all the odds and ends of furnishing and decorating the barn and now we had a dog and our new born baby in a second year.

Life was looking up, or was it? It wasn't. It was the calm before the storm.

I must warn you that the next chapter will be dark, and I don't mean that lights will be missing, I mean that the lights will go out completely. I won't take offence if you skip the next chapter but for this to be a full story and to end on a happy note with Chapter 22, the next chapter, chapter 20, had to be written.

Besides, if it helps you avoid my fate and saves just one person from going through what I went through it's worth writing Chapter 20.

Chapter 20 – The Destruction of A Family And Me

"Success is not final, failure is not fatal: it is the courage to continue that counts. When going through hell, keep going!"

Winston Churchill, Wartime Leader, Adventurer and Novelist.

When I think of hard times and the difficulties faced in life I try to put it in perspective. My Dad gave me something that his great uncle had made. It was a World War I brass shell case from a 25 pounder artillery gun. My great uncle had been ordered onto the worst battlefields in Europe during World War I. He had come upon the shell case and spent time carving names of the great battles he was involved in into the brass shell case before cutting the casing into flower shapes that he folded outwards.

The shell casing sits on my mantelpiece like four flowers coming out of one brass stem. The shell casing has held me in good stead in difficult times. It always reminds me that no matter how bad my situation is there are people who suffered worse. I don't mean that in a macabre way but in a perspective way. Things are never that bad really in the bigger picture of things.

If you want to skip this chapter you can do but I feel this chapter needs to be written because it's what happened, and it is the personal cost of building my own home, and without doubt the bleakest darkest situation I have ever faced. But this chapter needed including to appreciate the happier moments that follow and maybe even provide comfort to those builders going through difficult times in their own self-build.

I'll begin. The elation of a new-born child soon wore off. When you have a new-born baby it's great that everyone wants to visit, but mothers are usually exhausted and the house is usually a bomb site. Some of you will realise that everything is side-lined in order to ensure that the baby is looked after twenty-four hours a day, seven days a week. Normal day-to-day tasks were put on hold, almost seemingly forever. The best piece of advice that I received was as soon as the baby is asleep you should go to sleep. You can survive a surprisingly long period of time on adrenaline and no sleep but at some point the batteries need recharging.

My wife's batteries weren't being recharged. Help was coming from all sorts of agencies and with family coming to support us. However my wife was struggling. The usual ways of bolstering her moods were not possible whilst she was breastfeeding. Professionals came to support and eventually it was realised as well as everything else our baby was tongue-tied. Without a quick operation to release her tongue our little girl was unable to feed fully and was always hungry. She'd be persistently awake and being tongue-tied, constantly vomited due to gulping air down with her feeds.

The days passed and the weeks passed. My wife's moods were slipping away. She was trying her best but there was a pessimism about how she would cope in the future. All the persuasion in the world wasn't helping. When experts came and went things struggled to improve. Meals I prepared were barely touched and even her sister's favourite homemade ready meals were being ignored. Eventually the inevitable happened - my two weeks of paternity leave was over. Tired right through to the bone I returned to work leaving my wife with her sister.

I could see the life draining from my wife's face. I was now getting up early in the morning, feeding baby and mother, then doing a full day at work before racing home to cook tea, feed our baby and mother, feed and walk the dog, wash bottle paraphernalia and so on.

Then I'd drag myself up the stairs before collapsing in bed and getting up what seemed like every hour on the hour to feed our baby. We were tired. Very tired. My wife was getting more and more upset as she imagined anything and everything was going wrong.

On one particular day our baby took a turn for the worst and the midwife was due to visit. My baby still had issues from an infection she'd had in hospital in the womb as well as still tongue tied. We waited and waited, bleary eyed for the midwife to arrive. Tiredness was growing.

The midwife was now a new midwife and unlike the health visitors, the predecessor midwife and other visitors, she did not use the less obvious but longer, official drive to the barn. The new midwife had driven up the contentious shared drive way. The new midwife would be met and turned away by a furious Mrs Interfering.

When I saw the events unfold on the CCTV I saw red for the first time. I was at the end of my patience with Mrs Interfering. We had a sick, six day old baby and now Mrs Interfering was affecting our baby's life. She was willing to let my little child suffer. For the sake of stopping visitors travelling the five metres of the shared drive she'd allow my child to come to harm!

I was a vivid red. I raced out to save the midwife but it was too late, she had got in her car and had driven off at the instruction of Mrs Interfering. I raged. I shouted "Interfering!!" at the top of my voice, at her home. Mrs Interfering didn't appear. I shouted repeatedly "Mrs Interfering!". She still didn't appear.

However the police did appear. With sirens and lights flashing they attended in record time. They took me inside my barn. I sat down and told them what Mrs Interfering had done. The officer was here to arrest me for a clear breach of the peace. I was going to be taken away.

In the fall out I had one crucial lucky break. Luckily for me, the wife of one of the police officers had just had a baby. He understood where I was coming from and the exasperation I was feeling. Instead of an arrest, he said he'd speak to Mrs Interfering. The now parked police car and its flashing lights attracted help. The builder's wife came over to the barn to see me and she said would speak to Mrs Interfering.

My wife started crying. She cried all day. A release of upset came pouring out. She couldn't stop and there was nothing I could do to comfort her. Even the only person she'd ever listened to - her mum - could not calm her down. Her elderly mum came straight over from her home town six miles away. Finally, hours later, my wife calmed down and went into a much needed deep sleep.

Things were going from bad to worse. Within six weeks my wife, my baby and even my dog would leave me. They'd all be gone. My wife had had enough and left broken. I was stunned.

For the first time in my life, a mental state in my mind was beginning to affect me physically.

Within a few short months I had the official divorce petition posted to me. Attempts to visit my wife and child had failed. Requests to see my baby were delayed from day to day, then I'd be told I could see her the following week, then the following fortnight, then the following month. I was denied all access by my wife's family and despite knowing them for over five years and visiting regularly, they disappeared quickly and firmly behind closed doors.

At home my family were also disappearing. The dangers of the neighbours meant they visited much less often. My Dad and brother were feeling the pinch in the declining farming industry. My elderly father loved his job and worked all hours he could. He'd worked long hours since he left school at sixteen in the 1950s. My brother, however, was always My Dad suggested as my brother was always saying he was short of money and I had a good job that he was going to change his will. My dad duly obliged in order to help my brother.

He would, for the time being, inherit all of the farm and now my inheritance. I was disinherited and however it was broadcast, the whole village knew. Those who weren't fans of me, mentioned the black sheep status I was now carrying. Snide remarks were made to me anytime fellow villagers could. Gossip spread like wild fire - I was the one causing trouble - maybe I was - but the rumours evolved and exploded as news of an impending divorce also seeped out.

My wife had left, my family were leaving, and the neighbours were also ramping up the pressure.

The neighbours now wanted to sell a garage I owned. They wanted the garage I owned and which Mrs Interfering had for a yearly fee before the troubles, occupied decades before. Despite informing the estate agents I owned the garage, they freely advertised Mrs Interfering's home in the press with her garage listed and my garage listed alongside it too.

Eventually I was to be slammed again. Whilst at my parents' home not fifty metres from the barn, a visitor in a suit arrived. I signed for the parcel upon seeing my name. The bundle contained a legal collection of papers called, in law speak a 'paginated bundle'. I was to be sued by Mrs Interfering for fifty thousand pounds. Not just that, to avoid legal action she wanted money off each of us; my dad, brother and me, plus for me to surrender the title deeds to my garage.

The paginated bundle and news of impending legal action overshadowed our lives. On the eve of the stag do I had arranged for my brother's wedding, the physical state of my body was about to take effect. In the classroom I was starting to pass out. As much as I tried, I could not stand for more than a few minutes at a time before my vision blurred and my head felt very dizzy. My chest was tight and I was unable to breath. My line manager was called. Worried I was about to have a heart attack, I was given an immediate appointment with a doctor.

The tests showed I was missing heart beats. And missing lots of them. The doctor diagnosed ectopic heart beats. In some cases, ectopic beats can be dangerous. If your ectopic beats are dangerous your cardiologist will advise you of this. It is up to you to decide what treatment you want. In my case when I explained the plethora of incidents the doctor recommended rest or pills. The pills were severe and could make me impotent. The impotence bit didn't sound good but I couldn't rest - I had too much to think about.

I returned to work the following day with wires running up and down my chest to a heart monitor under my shirt. I needed to be at work to avoid going home. In the idle banter of the staff room I'd secretly become jealous of colleagues who could simply go home quietly each night. Jealous of how they talked about family time and doing mundane quiet tasks around the home.

In my world the bags were growing under my eyes like suitcases waiting for the next ride on the drama conveyor belt. People commented that I looked awful. I was dreading weekends on my own. Eventually I had a brief distraction on the horizon. I had a stag do to go to one weekend for my brother's wedding.

I went through lessons up to the weekend in a daze. I was starting to feel neither highs nor lows. Simply occupying my overactive mind was an issue. Eventually, the weekend of my brother's stag do arrived.

I raced home to a pre-packed suitcase before a trip to the doctors. The plan was, after the doctor visit, I'd set off on the next train for the stag do. I was late home due to traffic and ten minutes before I was due to see the doctor and get my heart monitor taken off. The doctor could then check the monitor and have its results printed out. I rang the surgery to apologise for a potential lateness but I would be there very soon. The police had different ideas however.

As I raced to get ready and head to the doctors, the local police sergeant and another officer appeared. Something else had now happened. My dad was ranting about the neighbours to the police. And unfortunately one officer had a body camera on and was videoing every word shouted. Anything could have been made of the potential video and angry words given in haste.

In some ways I must have been still connected in some way with the world as I calmed my Dad, persuaded the officers that whatever happened today was not our doing and headed to the doctors. The ten minutes of police interview saw my heart rate spike off the top of the chart.

"Healed", smiled the doctor.

"Your heart rate is up, so the good news is you are not missing heart beats now. Unfortunately, your heart rate is now the opposite and dangerously high", he quipped.

I had run to the surgery so as not to mess up other patients' appointment times and the police visit was still high on my mind. I fed this information to the doctor.

 "You probably want something to slow your heart down now", the doctor continued.

I didn't know if he was joking but based on the read-out he recommended further tests urgently and in the next few days. He mainly recommended things that could fix my heart but each remedy came with some pretty dramatic side effects.

"Rest and a quieter life is your best bet", he advised. "...And avoid more police visits".

In two years since the first building work on the barn had begun, I'd built a new home, got married and had a daughter. Now I was going to add to my life experiences. I was about to get sued, head to the divorce courts, fight to see my child in a family court and probably die from a lack of heart beats doing all of this.

Chapter 21 – My Day in Court, Many Courts

"You can get a divorce in England or Wales if you've been married at least a year and your relationship has permanently broken down. You must have a marriage that's legally recognised in the UK - this includes same-sex marriage. You must usually also have a permanent home in England or Wales. When you apply for a divorce you'll need to prove that your marriage has broken down. You'll need to give one or more of the following reasons:
- Adultery - Your husband or wife had sexual intercourse with someone else of the opposite sex. The law recognises the act of adultery as sexual intercourse between a man and a woman. You cannot give adultery as a reason if you lived together as a couple for six months after you found out about it.
- Unreasonable behaviour - Your husband or wife has behaved in such a way that you cannot reasonably be expected to live with them. This could include: physical violence, verbal abuse, such as insults or threats, drunkenness or drug-taking or refusing to pay for housekeeping.
- Desertion - Your husband or wife has left you; without your agreement, without a good reason, to end your relationship, for more than two years in the past two and a half years. Or;
- You've been separated for more than two years - You can apply for a divorce if you've been separated for more than two years and both agree to the divorce".

Adapted from The Family Court, www.gov.uk, 2017.

Generally speaking a divorce is a conspicuous way of destroying your finances and losing any property you've built. This is regardless of whether it's been acquired before or after you got married, unless of course you are a canny Scotsman and got married in Scotland, in which case under Scottish law the judge can only share out assets accumulated after you got married and not before.

When the divorce petition from my ex-wife landed through the letter box, I was reminded of our wedding service; dropping the ring once is bad enough if you are superstitious, however, dropping it twice must mean something crazy will happen. Now the one I once loved was going to pay a lot of smart, ruthless people to smash me emotionally and financially. I also fumed at the "love you till death do us part" bit too. Another wedding vow broken.

Incidentally, when my brother's wedding service began, the vicar who had performed my marriage service mistakenly and repeatedly referred to my brother's bride with my ex-wife's name. The more he realised his dreadful error the more he called my brother's wife the wrong name and turned increasingly red faced with embarrassment. The vicar was a very charismatic individual and that helped him 'get away with it' otherwise the ruffled feathers of the congregation would have been the least of his worries. The vicar has now since retired but I'm going off task here.

The divorce begins with one person saying that they want to get divorced and put this intention in the correct form. As my solicitor advised, there is no point fighting a divorce application because the other person doesn't want to be with you. If they did love you, they wouldn't have filled the form in and sent off their five hundred pound fee either. If you fight the divorce petition, a judge can simply say that the relationship has broken down due to irreconcilable differences and award a divorce anyway.

If you are a sensible couple, you would probably sit down and decide how you want your possessions dividing up. You would aim to award the money in a way for each side to enjoy a reasonable standard of living similar to how you both were before you met.

For a mother in court however the odds are in her favour. If you have a child, no court rightly wants to see the child homeless. In the UK, it's usually the father who moves out and he may end up still having to pay the mortgage even after he has left, or at least until the youngest child is out of full-time education. I agree that your child should be your main priority. It's only right that the little ones need a good place to stay, as they will have suffered enough during a divorce to scar them for many years to come. In the meantime a father could live in a tent or camper van depending on what little income was left for them.

If you can't decide how to split up your belongings then you need to go to court and a first hearing is where the major points are heard from both sides. This is called an FDR – First Dispute Resolution hearing. Your cases for who should get what is discussed with a judge and who then advises in a non-binding way. The idea is that as sensible adults you should be able to go and decide between yourselves how best to divide your possessions with just a little refereeing that is.

If you can't come to a sensible decision the judge will conduct a second, final hearing which will be legally binding. At the final hearing, the judge will make the decision on how best to divide the assets based on the needs of each former partner. It's usually a myth that things are divided 50/50. If you take a property, for example, you take the value of property, you deduct any mortgage outstanding, and then divide up the remaining money or equity based on what's considered fairest after the housing needs of both partners are taken into consideration.

I know what you're thinking and I thought this too. Bolt holes, off-shore bank accounts, buying expensive antiques to sell later. Don't start hiding assets in other people's names or going on a spending spree. As part of the divorce you need to disclose on a special form what you own and what you owe to others. You have to state and evidence how much you earn and what your true assets are. You need three months' worth of bank statements going back in time to prove what sort of expenditure and levels of savings you have. If you get creative with your numbers and get caught out, the judge is well within his or her rights to award everything to your former partner. And if you choose to spend all of your money you could be taking out a loan to pay for legal help. As a rough ballpark figure for the non-suicidal who want a solicitor; the average bill for divorce legal fees starts at around six thousand pounds and spirals quickly upwards from there. That bill is for a solicitor to handle things professionally, carefully and with brain power throughout the process on your behalf.

Once you have completed your divorce you won't be able to tell anyone what happened. You'll be bound by court rules of non-disclosure. Boasting or disclosing all of the gory details of a divorce case in the nearest pub could land you in trouble by being prosecuted for a breach of court confidentiality. It is treated as a serious issue if any of the divorce details sneak out so don't go posting any heated Facebook rants or arrange for billboard advertising outside your ex's office block, for example.

I was lucky regarding my home. For my ex-wife, the idea of living in my home next to my family and the neighbours probably meant I got to keep my home. Like most divorced home owners, I had to pay out to legally end all financial commitments to my ex-wife forever. You will have guessed I kept the barn and had to pay out my ex by seeing the pictures at the end of this book so I'm not giving anything away that you wouldn't have worked out for yourself.

There's not a lot else I can say other than it is normal to lie awake at night worried about where you are going to live. Whilst in that phrase 'open wound' you'll wonder if you'll be paying for your ex's mortgage until you drop dead or your children are old enough to leave full-time education or your ex-wife leaves the UK.

One of the most important things I had to figure out was how I went about getting access to my little daughter. You'll find most of your friends will split themselves between yourself and your former partner. Then there was always going to be a small group of friends who will sit on the garden fence and be friends with both sides. It was through one of these latter group of friends that enabled me to see my little daughter growing up and she was growing fast. The family courts are effective however they do take a long time to work. In my case it took a year in order to get access to my daughter. I missed most of the nappy changing and bottle feeding stages but luckily got access in time to see her move from crawling to walking.

To start to apply for access to your own child you first must go to an independent mediator. If an agreement can be made about child custody and access arrangements then ace! They'll ask a solicitor to rubber stamp and make the agreement binding. However if no agreement can be made, you apply with a C100 form to the family court. The documents you fill in are copied three times. Then the forms, along with your cheque for two hundred and eighty pounds, head off to your nearest court for an appointment scheduling. Again like a divorce procedure, you have a first non-binding hearing with a judge to discuss the key issues around accessing your child in a way convenient to both parties. If you fail to reach an agreement, then it's back for a final hearing where experts such as social workers, your statement, your ex's statement plus interviews in court are made before a judge. Then the judge hands down his legally binding verdict.

For legal reasons I can't go into the details but it's safe to say that I went through every hoop and loop possible. It's no court guided secret that I had to prove myself in many, many ways to satisfy the judges it was a good idea for my little girl to see me. You must however keep your feelings under control. You have to remember you're now lumped in with crazy mothers and abusive fathers and the court will expect anything and everything because they don't know you from Adam. I'm sure Adam is a really good guy but you'll have to prove yourself worthy of your child.

Very few fathers or even mothers will have a certificate to say that they can change a baby's nappy to a high standard. Fewer still will have to go through the humiliation and humbling experience of meeting their daughter again for the first time through a contact centre. A contact centre is a supervised play centre were Mummy and Daddy don't have to meet and see each other. It's a way of reintroducing the absent parent back into the child's life. I had to undergo various workshop sessions in the quest to see my daughter. Most notably I achieved an 'excellent' rating (from the social workers) for my daddy and daughter relationship building skills in the contact centre. I was gutted I didn't get an actual certificate for my certificate box but success meant that I was able to start bringing my daughter to other places, before finally bringing her back to her family home and introducing overnight stays.

Needless to say, my proudest moment in any of the numerous court hearings or building works were eclipsed by one moment. The tests I withstood faded into insignificance compared to one amazing moment. That amazing moment was when I finally brought my daughter back home for the first time after her year away. When my daughter returned and I carried her little body and smiling face back to her first ever home in this world, I was the extreme opposite of the previous chapter. I was winning again and my treasure was back playing in the room I had designed years before for her.

When you start visiting different courts so many times and have had contact with more than five of my ex-wife's barristers, six legal practices and a plethora of social workers you become pretty good at being organised. I considered renaming my address 'Fort Turner' as the council ask you what the name of your newly built home will be. I thought of Turner Halls, Turner Cottage or something that ensured my place in history. In the end I wearily settled for Number 11 of my street. The numbers of opponents would increase as the pressures on Fort Turner increased. The pressures on the little money I had left was intense. I was at the extreme end of my finances. There were countries with smaller debts than me.

If you're interested in saving your money, you'll get good at representing yourself in courts.   You can save yourself two hundred pounds an hour for a solicitor or five hundred pounds per hour and upwards for a barrister. A barrister or a solicitor's time pressures mean they'll barely glance over your case before heading in to see a judge who will then make earth-shattering decisions about your life. For such a brief service, their prices will look like extortion when you can ring your solicitor for fifty pounds a call for advice and then represent yourself. You'll also find other people in similar trouble gravitate towards you in the staff room at work. They'll know to ask you legal questions as you become part of the unlucky divorcee club.

The divorcee club, impromptu friends in need or 'single dads for justice' club will expand around you. Your knowledge of court and law will also grow through experience. You can find a wealth of information on the internet but unfortunately nothing is better than the experience of a good solicitor and his or her brain power. You just have to pay for it and the rest you'll learn through 'on-the-job training'.

I was now well trained. After the hurdles of divorce and child custody, dealing with the neighbour's solicitor was actually surprisingly easy to master. I'm proud to tell you that they lost their demand to extort money and my garage from me and my family. It wasn't through any particular genius.

The paginated bundle they sent was the main cause of their failed legal challenge. A paginated bundle is a document that you send to court to sustain and disclose a claim's evidence against someone. Luckily, key things were made up and other things were physically impossible. On one particular date I was meant to be conducting some heinous crime to the neighbour but that date coincided with a holiday. My holiday booking details confirmed that I wasn't even in the country on a range of dates I was meant to be raising hell in the neighbourhood. One of my favourites from their claims was a 'snooping' charge. I was meant to be snooping around the bushes of the neighbour in order to cause a disturbance. In reality, the date the neighbour chose was the same day I was getting married and thoughts of the neighbours couldn't have been any further from my mind.

When the paginated bundle arrived I rang my legal insurance and forwarded the bundle on to them. Following a few letters the challenge was withdrawn. Mrs Interfering's long standing legal bluff faded away.

Mrs Interfering eventually moved home one day without giving any notice to any of her neighbours or local friends we knew, she quietly slipped away.

Money was wasted and lost for both families on a scale that still brings a tear to my eyes when I think about it. The neighbour dispute was a shame because both families had happily known each other for decades. The relationship only imploded as I tried to build my home out of the barn behind her house.

Ultimately falling out with people doesn't gain very much. I've seen first-hand how much it costs and how much it cost me in my personal life. I can't imagine either of us enjoyed living next to each other but if it is ever to happen again in another life I'd hope we would get on better for our mistakes.

Chapter 20 was a difficult chapter to write but it was a necessary one. I was down further than I ever thought it was possible. Now I was finally getting back up on my feet. I learnt from a whole new experience about the law, the legal system and ways to keep myself occupied and positive. Like Winston Churchill recommended when our tiny island of Great Britain stood alone against all the horrors of World War II - his key recommendation - no matter what, keep going. He was right, I had learnt it the hard way but Churchill was right. Things were now going to be much brighter.

Things were very much better and my journey as a home builder was almost coming to a happy end. Remember I said at the beginning this would end with a happy ending, we are almost there.

Chapter 22 – The Sunshine After The Rain

"Optimism is the faith that leads to achievement. Nothing can be done without hope and confidence. Don't wait for it to happen. Make it happen. Make your own future. Make your own hope. Make your own love. And whatever your beliefs, honour your creator, not by passively waiting for grace to come down from upon high, but by doing what you can to make grace happen... yourself, right now, right down here on Earth".

Helen Keller 1880-1968 American author, political activist, and lecturer. First deaf-blind person to earn a Bachelor of Arts Degree.

When I was small and still at school I remember thinking about what life would be like when I was older. Really older; say twenty or thirty years of age, or even forty, because that would be really old. I had a mental picture about a job I might do. I'd probably have a car and a house. I'd probably have a season ticket for my local football team. I'd probably enjoy a pint of beer, which at the moment as a child I still hated the taste of. And I would probably have a wife and two children. And then, my small child's mind reasoned, I'd probably have grandchildren and then die.

What I didn't expect were the twists and turns of life. I now had a daughter but no wife. I was also about to enter new, uncharted territory; after a five-year-old relationship and a very, very, short marriage I was about to head back out into the Wild West of the dating scene. The old adage that all is fair in love and war was about to be tested once more.

Luckily however, I wouldn't be going out into the dating Wild West without some support. I think one of the features of my life that I've always been most blessed with is good, solid friends. My friends had helped keep me sane as well as making me laugh by making light of anything and everything. When I couldn't see my daughter until a year of court battles had finished – the ever helpful boys' response was 'here she is on Facebook' on her Mum's profile. For some fathers that would have broken them but coming from these 'degenerates' as Sam affectionately called them, it was almost funny. I say almost.

The plan to get round town would be similarly supported from my Thirsty Thursday drinking group, I had four friends who for a variety of reasons were about to head out with me to tame the Wild West and search for a new girl.

Two of the boys were single by choice. They mostly preferred the bachelor lifestyle and to be honest I found their stories and nights out antics both fascinating and amusing. By contrast the other two boys had singleton status thrust upon them without any choice. Both 'thrusted' boys worked long hours and often did night shifts at work in order to provide for their other halves. Unfortunately, whilst they were busy, their wives were even busier - with other boyfriends. The infidelity must have been devastating. Even more devastating as the boys were paying for the comfy lifestyles their wives enjoyed but living like slaves themselves. At least my ex-wife hadn't cheated on me, she'd simply had enough and left.

It was time to head round town for drinks at the weekends. Time to join clubs and to do new things. In our twenties, it seemed that we chased the girls, now in our thirties, it seemed like the girls were chasing us. I presumed that it was due to the biological clock of ladies wanting to settle down. Harry was more cynical - it was because of the booty he had built up during his working career. Andrew had another perspective. Andrew put it down to now being a higher earner as he could fund more nights out. Put simply more places meant more girls and therefore more opportunities due to our now older, and bigger salaries. He was a fan of the *numbers game* of dating as many girls as possible and he was a relentless spender on the social scene.

Technology had improved by this new dating era, no longer were dating apps the preserve of potential serial killers and dateless wonders. Dating apps had become mainstream. Andrew was a massive fan of apps like Tinder and Plenty of Fish. He had turned dating into a computer game and always had several 'prospects' on the go at the same time. In fielding such a large number of potential dates and girlfriends, he employed a systematic, almost production line approach. The production line approach involved a wide variety of prewritten template text messages, emails with 'insert name here' spaces and other dating strategies he could fire out at a moment's notice.

On many nights out Andrew would be in a conundrum. There would be hundreds of real girls walking past our table in a pub. The girls would have spent hours getting dressed and made up ready especially to talk to guys like Andrew. However, Andrew was oblivious most nights to the real girls around him. Instead, he tended to his virtual world, starting online conversations, setting up dates and chasing leads up and down the entire county. In turning the dating game into a computer game, the only emotion I ever saw from Andrew involved a pretty girl on Tinder called Jessica who he showed to his friends. Ryan was quick on the uptake and asked Andrew for a closer look. Andrew made the mistake of passing the phone to Ryan. Before Andrew had realised, Ryan had gone past the photo of the pretty Jessica and was feverously pressing the 'Like' button to anyone and everyone. Likes were given particularly to the girls he knew Andrew would deem *really, really* ugly. Andrew almost cried as the software started to match him now with girls the size of buses or those who had not been blessed by Mother Nature's beauty. By contrast, Tom had a more 'real world' approach to dating.

Tom was strictly about the numbers. His philosophy about dating was 'fling enough mud and some sticks'. The Tom plan was simply to approach as many girls as possible. Tom had frequently collected a lot of phone numbers in an evening. Or even disappeared at some point during the evening - presumably as a good soul who wanted to help some girl cut down the cost of a taxi home by sharing it. In Tom's dating philosophy of talking to anyone and everyone in the real world and having the widest social circle possible had a lot of plus points. However Tom's strategy was not without its own pitfalls.

Tom's 'numbers' strategy enabled a great prank to be played. Tom frequently met so many girls he did not know who was who. One day when he left his mobile phone on the table in the bar, we changed one of our numbers to a girl's name and duly arrange a date with him. A few crafty text messages later and Tom was about to go on a date with one of us. It should have been suspicious when Martin kept leaving the bar to text, or when he received the perfect picture we sent him of a girl taken from the internet. Or the fact that the 'girl' wanted to meet in one of the bars we hit every Thirsty Thursday. The warning signs were obvious. Nonetheless Tom was caught out and not impressed when on the night we all emerged instead of his date.

Dating seemed easier these days. I did say earlier that it tended to be girls in the 30s who now started to chase us. I missed out one vital detail. In my opinion some of these girls were single for a reason.

One girl I met a few times was a friend of a friend. She ended up with the name 'Ghost Girl' by the Thirsty Thursday mob – but not for the reason you're thinking. Ghost Girl was a very pretty, vivacious girl, bordering on the wild and unpredictable side. She came round to the barn one night for tea and just as things were about to get interesting, she started having an argument.

She started shouting at an empty sofa, "What are you looking at? Yes, you?"

Even in the romantic candlelight I had set up, it was clear there was nobody there.

"Who are you shouting at?" I asked.

"I'm shouting at those three looking at us now", she said sternly. "One of them is walking towards you now".

I don't usually believe in ghosts but the girl's conviction was so real I started to get goose bumps. The hairs on the back of my arm started to stand up. A small amount of alcohol had now quietened my rational side and I started to wonder what had happened in the three-hundred-year-old history of the barn.

I waited intently to see whether some ghost or apparition would appear. Eventually, it was time to put a film on and forget the candles.

Nothing ghostly happened and my encounters with the Ghost Girl came to an end. She moved into my friends' dating folklore.

Dating is quite an adventure. It is often a chance to experience someone else's life to understand a whole new different way of doing things; from cooking meals at the barn, to days out, I was privileged to get a glimpse into someone else's world and if it sounded good and felt good I started to date.

One girl I dated was a beautiful nurse I'd met on a night out. She had long blond hair with blue eyes and we had a lot in common. I had converted a dilapidated building into my home and she was doing the same with a former council house that she'd bought. She did a tough job as a front-line nurse. Some of her stories from the accident and emergency ward were hair raising at times, funny on occasions and sometimes touchingly sentimental. She helped families and patients at their most vulnerable hours of need. She was great to get on with but the hours were horrendous. Sometimes she was on night shifts so she could only visit at night time, midweek. As my day would be finishing, hers would be starting and teaching bleary-eyed after being up all night was a challenge. Ultimately, we stayed friends and eventually she wanted to travel and moved abroad for a higher wage.

As you'd expect people have different personalities. One girl I dated was very chatty with a dry sense of humour. I took her to the beer festival where we met my friends and hers. She had a go at shooting arrows on the archery display. The amateur archery enthusiasts showed her how to hold a bow and fire a real, steel-tipped arrow. It was very brave to put on that sort of entertainment at a beer festival where there was a high possibility of people shooting themselves or having some sort of alcohol-related accident. Inevitably, Charlotte slipped with the bow and with a dry sense of humour said she'd sue the organisers as she laughed off the pain. In full view of the waiting crowd, the archery stand was packed up and the volunteers rushed away. An oblivious Charlotte wandered back off to the beer tent.

A year later, and things were moving on. I was now heading for two years since my wife left. Two years where a lot had changed.

Things were picking up. And I meant that literally. I had by this time progressed through all the different court orders and now I was picking up my daughter regularly each week and bringing her home.

My little daughter had her own bedroom stuffed to the rafters with toys, cuddly bears, her wardrobe full of clothing and all the other little possessions she was collecting. The bedroom had been designed for a child. The bedroom was on the first floor right next to the glass walkway that linked the two halves of the barn together. To avoid waking up my little daughter, the room had been designed with two ceiling-to-floor glass panels so it meant I could look in on the room without opening the door and waking her up. It also meant my daughter could look down into the living room below and her small room felt so much larger.

My daughter was also making good use of my garage near to the barn. Her favourite toys such as her tricycle and her Wendy house were stored there. There was no longer just one set of my clothes hanging up in the barn. Finally, next to my coats and shoes, were tiny pairs of trainers and shoes for a little 2-year-old, little coats and jackets, and other little person paraphernalia. It had taken a full year to go through the courts to get access to her, but now I had a permanent, regular little visitor who would brighten my day up every week. This situation was about to improve even further.

My brother and his fiancée needed somewhere to stay whilst they did up the farmhouse to live in. They stayed at my house. They weren't at home very often but it was nice to have company after now two years of living on my own. A girl involved in the barn this way was fine. However, when it came to a girlfriend of mine living in the house, I was very much of the 'once bitten, twice shy' perspective to a girl moving in with me.

It was now getting on for two years of living alone. Over the years, I'd said many, many times to friends and family that no girlfriend was ever moving into my home. I would happily date someone but we'd live separately. After three years, this fear of living with someone again after my ex-wife was, heaven forbid, about to change.

One night in Clitheroe, I saw a couple of girls and one looked very familiar to me. I looked a couple of times, racking my brains to think who it could be. I know, I thought to myself, she's a friend's wife. I'll go over and say "hello" briefly so I don't look rude.

I approached the girls and said "Hello". I asked the friend's wife how she was, how the kids and Danny were. The conversation was a bit stilted. Then I realised. She had absolutely no idea who or what I was talking about. Red faced I apologised, wished the girls a good night and re-joined my friends.

That night was a big night out as one of the boys was celebrating. We were also meeting one of the boys' new girlfriend for the first time. It was a policy of best behaviour and no inappropriate banter whenever we were introduced to somebody's new girlfriend. It was reasoned that the 'real us' shouldn't come out until a girl felt sufficiently comfortable with us. However, we always behaved when Rod and Lee's partners came out so Tom had an easy night that night. Safely things were going well for Tom despite the boys slowly slipping out of control as they continued to drink around town.

Three bars later, however, the cocktails and the shots were coming out and the noise level was going up a gear. The jokes and loudness were back and Tom's girlfriend had been sufficiently interviewed by all of us to deem her as 'Good'. Which unfortunately, meant that the 'real' us was now starting to come out.

Suddenly, I saw a girl who was friend of mine - Lauren. Lauren was alongside the same two girls I had a mistakenly identified earlier on that night. The girl of mistaken identity was smiling at me and listening to something Lauren was saying to her. I knew it must have been something funny because she was now laughing. Knowing Lauren, I thought I had better go over and defend what had been said about me. I went over.

I found out the mistaken identity girl was called Joanna.

I bought Joanna a drink and we got chatting about the people we knew and didn't know. We talked about where she had grown up, what she did job wise and what brought her to Clitheroe. She wore a beautiful dress and the hint of summer was still evident from the sunglasses still resting on her head from earlier in the day.

Her friends and mine joined each other and we wandered off together from bar to bar. It was a very drunken night and we partied into the small hours until the Theatre of Dreams. The Theatre of Dreams was a name stolen from Manchester United's home ground. Despite most of us never having been fans of Manchester United, it seemed a funny euphemism for the last ditch, dive nature of our final bar. It was the bar that opened the latest into the night and most drinkers heading around town usually finished the night in there. Everyone was too cool to say they enjoyed the place but secretly everyone did. Despite everyone we knew using the Theatre of Dreams as the last chance saloon to meet people, it was popular and lively. Most visitors secretly enjoyed throwing caution and usually drinks to the wind as they partied into the early hours. Within the Theatre of Dreams, on the loud and jostling dance floor, the mystery girl gave me her phone number. Joanna was happily added to my phone.

At the end of the night it was like a scene from Cinderella. Joanna and her friends headed off to get their carriage or in this case a last taxi home before the early morning price hikes. I was now left with a phone number that I hoped in this case worked. I had given out more than my fair share of dodgy numbers with the last digit changed. I hoped Cinderella hadn't done the same.

The following evening, I reached for my phone and I gave Joanna a call. As the phone rang I thought about the now vague, alcohol tinged memories of the evening. Funnily enough I didn't feel nervous as I rang to say "hello". I didn't feel apprehension as I chatted to see if she enjoyed the night and to ask her if she was free *sometime* to catch up over a coffee or a drink. I remembered, out of all of the faces I'd seen, Joanna had stood out from the crowd and I loved the warmth of her personality.

Two days later, we met up at the picturesque and medieval Mitton Hall just three miles from home. Its evening fire and warm bar made a wonderful and special backdrop to meeting the mystery girl from Saturday night. Meeting up with Joanna and sharing an evening over coffee was planned. Off I went to see if she matched my now sober memories of my first encounter with her.

As Joanna walked through the door, and with a smile on her face, she confidently walked up to me and I gave her a kiss on the cheek. She was as beautiful as I had remembered. Harry said I should have got a sneaky photo of her so I could 'judge' her the day afterwards when I was sober. It was a shallow idea but I was tempted – just in case my memory had played a trick on me. I needn't have worried. She was as fun and beautiful as I remembered her. I ordered her a drink and we sank down in the big sofa together in front of the open, wood fire.

I had no idea how great that chance encounter in a bar would be. But I do now. I was always told that great people make their own luck and that the shallow believe in chance. I knew that the last few years of difficulty had been good preparation. Joanna had a similar experience of working on a self-build home and as well as the world beyond building, we had a common bond. The disasters which seemed painful at the time were actually interesting and at times funny. They breathed life into conversations and allowed a conversation to flow in all sorts of directions. Our building tales were the root from which mutual understanding that later fun, adventure and time shared together would emanate. The chance encounter was more than just good luck –

Joanna was a beautiful find with a personality that gave hope for the future.

Three years later there are now new things hanging up in the hallway. A man's set of coats and a little girl's set of clothing is now joined by a third set of possessions - those of a girlfriend. Far from being afraid of sharing a home with a girlfriend, things have moved on. Semi-serious jokes about creating a bachelor pad, full of beer and parties, with live-in buddy Josh, had gone. The barn and I had a renewed hope and purpose.

It's funny how new things appearing around the barn now give me a warm smile; Joanna's scarf draped over the back of a sofa, a perfume bottle left on the kitchen table or a cuddly Mickey Mouse with its oversized hands sat on a sofa ready to watch TV. The barn is now a home. A home dotted with a little girl's toys, a girlfriend's belongings and all the things I had accumulated over the years of my life, mingled together with them.

Despite my fears and determination to live alone, the barn is now a home again. It's as busy and bustling with friends and family coming and going as I hoped it would be. The dreams I had almost a decade ago, when as a young man I first started drawing designs to turn a dilapidated building into a home, were coming true. That young man with a dream in his eye is now greyer. But I think he'd be proud of what his older self has achieved.

Despite the odds, I have succeeded.

Chapter 23 – Building – A Reflection On A Hell of A Ride

"Home is where our story begins... Home is the starting place of love, hope and dreams. The magic thing about home is that it feels good to leave, and it feels even better to come back. Home is where love resides, memories are created, friends always belong, and laughter never ends. A house is made of bricks and beams. A home is made of hopes and dreams. Home is not a place...it's a feeling".

F. Scott Fitzgerald, regarded as one of the greatest American writers of the 20th century 1896-1940.

July 2018

Today is a sunny day. It's literally boiling. Today, the Ribble Valley is firmly gripped by an extraordinary period of super-hot, sunny weather. The garden which was once rubble strewn and bare is now green and in flower. The lawn gently slopes away to grand views overlooking the Ribble Valley. The trees are in full leaf and the sky is a very clear, holiday blue.

The barn is complete now. Swings and a little slide for a toddler sit where crates of concrete blocks once rested. The window frames are painted and the windows are now open to release heat from the sun kissed barn. In the garden my little daughter is playing with her dolls in her wendy house and tending to her flowers – dandelions and daisies to you or I. She's waiting for her grandparents to arrive. Tea will be on the barbecue this evening and we'll eat 'al fresco' in the garden. I can see through the kitchen window, my girlfriend has her blue check apron on and is busily preparing chicken kebabs and skewers for the barbecue.

I can sit here in the garden with a smile on my face.

Building a home is difficult. You have followed my story through more losses than victories. The numbers of this story say it all; in the end, there were visits by twenty-eight police officers and dealings with six different legal practices. I had beaten five barristers and overcome five council enforcement investigations. I dealt with three different banks and took out six different credit cards. I dealt with over 60 different suppliers, faced arrest, wore a heart monitor and had to stop a potential gas explosion. There were other things such as... in fact, to be honest who cares? I have a wonderful home and that was my aim.

But what is a home? In my opinion I'd say it's more than just simply bricks and cement. Some of you might say its blood, sweat and tears. Others would say it is a way of losing your sanity. Some would believe it's a great investment in the future or a way to make money. For me, a home is much more than any of these. To some extent all of these are true but a home is how a building makes you feel.

Your home is an opportunity to decorate in the way you feel fit and to do things your way. Few people will have more input into your home than yourself. A home makes you feel like you belong. Whenever I've had a good day or bad day, the barn is the place where I retreat to. From the cosy sofa time in front of the fire to the soft bed, I now feel I belong here. I also feel the home has a purpose as well. We can cook, eat and sleep here. To the self-builder the home serves to remind you that you're capable of more than you think. It's like a special day every day in more ways than one.

Last Christmas time serves as a great example. Christmas time was very special - especially with a toddler running around the house. I can still remember the magic of Christmas when I was the same age as my daughter. I was determined to make sure that this home delivered the same Christmas excitement that I had experienced in my childhood in my parents' farmhouse some 30 years ago.

Christmas was exciting. Lights and especially flashing lights were the biggest excitement to my little daughter. Very quickly we had placed lights up around the house and upon the Christmas tree. With an open plan living room, there was no limit to the height for the Christmas tree. Baubles were placed on the tree from the glass walkway above and from the living room below. For those awkward to reach places in-between, baubles were placed on the tree by my daughter's little hands as she sat on my shoulders. My little daughter's bedroom was alive very early on Christmas morning. Her little face peered down through the ceiling to floor, glass window of her room. She could see the Christmas tree and presents below. The barn came alive over a big table of Christmas dinner, present swapping and festive celebrations.

When you build your own home you can look back over things such as Christmas. You can be proud. You created some of these 'forever' memories. Without your building of brick and cement, the memories couldn't exist. My girlfriend cooked the Christmas dinner and my daughter created the handprint paintings for the kitchen fridge door. These events give the barn memories which makes it more than just a house – it's now a home.

There is just one more thing I'd like to share with you before we say goodbye. It's a poem that's been on the fridge door ever since I moved in. It's a poem I grew to know well during my building adventures. I used it to gather comfort and inspiration from its verses. The poem was written by a wartime Spitfire hero and a world famous author. I want to share its gems with other would-be self-builders:

If you can keep your head when all about you
 Are losing theirs and blaming it on you,
If you can trust yourself when all men doubt you,
 But make allowance for their doubting too.
If you can wait and not be tired by waiting,

 Or being lied about, don't deal in lies,
 Or being hated, don't give way to hating,
  And yet don't look too good, nor talk too wise:

If you can dream—and not make dreams your master;
 If you can think—and not make thoughts your aim;
If you can meet with Triumph and Disaster,
 And treat those two impostors just the same;
If you can bear to hear the truth you've spoken
 Twisted by knaves to make a trap for fools,
Or watch the things you gave your life to, broken,
 And stoop and build 'em up with worn-out tools:

If you can make a heap of all your winnings
 And risk it on one turn of pitch-and-toss,
And lose, and start again at your beginnings
 And never breathe a word about your loss;
If you can force your heart and nerve and sinew
 To serve your turn long after they are gone,
And so hold on when there is nothing in you
 Except the Will which says to them: "Hold on!"

If you can talk with crowds and keep your virtue,
 Or walk with Kings—nor lose the common touch,
If neither foes nor loving friends can hurt you,
 If all men count with you, but none too much;
If you can fill the unforgiving minute
 With sixty seconds' worth of distance run,
Yours is the Earth and everything that's in it,
 And—which is more—you'll be a Man, my son!

The poem is by Rudyard Kipling. He was inspired by heroics he saw in
battle and penned the poem in 1910. When you build your own home,

there will be times when you doubt yourself or people doubt you. You can't just live on dreams alone, there comes a point when you need to put these dreams into actual deeds and reality or you waste away your time with your head in the clouds. The hardest part for me of building my own home was the risk. As Rudyard Kipling pointed out, people don't like to hear you do too well because it challenges their reasons for not doing something. And you certainly don't want people to know if you failed because you'll never hear the end of it. You have to be willing to take a risk. You don't know if you're going to be successful but you need to try your very best or regret it later. For me, Kipling is wise. You need to meet disaster and success almost as if two are the same. Panic and running around screaming helps nobody but neither does boasting. Boasting and screaming is reserved for poor horror movies and not for winning over the hearts and minds of suppliers, supporters or friends.

Some people search in horoscopes or take up yoga to find themselves. Or go sailing around the world until the money runs out in order to discover themselves. Forget that, find a ruin of a building or better still a fresh plot of land and build a home. Get yourself in deep and hope for the best. You are capable of more than you think. As Hunter S. Thompson put it so well:

"Life shouldn't be a journey to the grave with the intention of arriving safely in a pretty and well preserved body, but rather to skid in broadside in a cloud of smoke, thoroughly used up, totally worn out and loudly proclaiming what a ride!"

Whatever your aim is in life don't let dreams fade away. Dig deep and breathe life in to your hopes and aspirations. Promise me that you won't give up even if you feel it, even if people tell you to quit or even if people dislike you for doing something. You deserve your right to dream and to your future.

I'm going to finish my story. I'm going to get back to my sunny garden and enjoy the sun whilst it lasts. I've got my little girl who's now sitting on my knee looking at my laptop. She wants to show me the daisies she's picked. My girlfriend is smiling from the kitchen window and hinting I should be warming the barbecue up. Grandparents are arriving shortly for tea and drinks need chilling.

This is the story of triumph over disaster, success over defeat and the in between of building your own home. Wherever I go and whatever happens now, there's a place in this world where an average Joe, his girlfriend and his daughter will be forever at home.

I'm an average Joe, and this is the story of the house that Dave built. It's the story of how his life got turned upside down...for the better. ☺

Images from the build

The barn conversion at the new roof stage.

The barn conversion and centuries-old beams and stone slates.

A time saving solution to wheeling in concrete foundations mix.

The trench that carries the utilities and knifed the farm fields in half.

Mrs Interfering's road block in progress.

Me, not one of my best photos, taken from a passing digger. Here I am briefly resting in between hauling concrete blocks through the mud. This was before the monsoon hit!

A building is cement and bricks but a home is people and memories.

Football on the walkway linking the barn together.

The future is exciting.

My girlfriend with my little daughter spotted in the background.

Other titles due out soon are:

'A Dishonest Code' - more details at www.adishonestcode.com

'A Thoroughly Modern Treasure Hunt' - more details at www.adishonestcode.com

Other releases are available from Big Hits Publishing - more details at www.bighitspublishing.com

About The Author

David lives in the relative quiet of the Ribble Valley, Lancashire with his girlfriend and family. He is still a keen building and DIY enthusiast but earns his living as a Head of Department in a school. He enjoys all things aircraft related and is currently learning to sail. He thanks you very much for reading his book and hopes you will read his latest book when it comes out – 'A Thoroughly Modern Treasure Hunt'.

More details are at www.athoroughlymoderntreasurehunt.com

A big thank you to you the reader!

Printed in Great Britain
by Amazon